IN PRAISE

*I went to University for 6 years part time to get a Bachelor of Business (Accounting)
and now it turns out I've learnt more useful real business management skills in
6 hours through reading this book!* If you run a business, you need the The
6-hour MBA. *I will be recommending it to anyone/everyone I know. If you
are part of any business, you need* The 6-hour MBA.

Jon Willis, CEO – CVP Events, Film & Television

*I recommend this book not as a substitute for an MBA, but to MBAs themselves.
Experienced managers, fledgling entrepreneurs, and students of management
will benefit from the practical wisdom, rigorous thinking, engaging and pithy
style, and profound observations. Mr. Coutts, a master at turning around
struggling and failing organizations, has distilled the fundamentals of successful
management into a straightforward, comprehensive set of principles. The book
never deviates from its focus on matters that drive organizational effectiveness
over the long, sustainable term. Indeed, you will not look at customers, employees
and cash quite the same way again, nor fail to thoughtfully challenge the latest
management fad or theory.* The 6-hour MBA *provides a strong foundation
that will help good people make good decisions, which better the organization
and the communities it serves.*

Professor Robert Widing
Dean of the Macquarie Graduate School of Management
Macquarie University

IN PRAISE OF THE 6-HOUR MBA

This book is precisely what Lou is all about: remarkably conceptual, eminently practical, profoundly thoughtful and constantly provocative. This blend of practical usable information and conceptual frameworks that challenge and push the reader (and user) is what many of us strive for, but rarely achieve. Lou's ability to look at a specific task or project closely and then to step back and frame the larger picture before returning to a specific task at hand is unequalled, and enlightening. I would recommend this book highly, for those who "do" management, as well as for those who "think" of new and novels ways of organizational effectiveness.

N. Mohan Reddy
Dean and Albert J. Weatherhead III Professor of Management
Weatherhead School of Management
Case Western Reserve University

This book is a wonderful introduction to what really matters in business and management. In an era when management is becoming overly specialised and technical, knowing how to focus on the basics is becoming harder to achieve. Coutts shows how, and how many of the answers to management are far more concerned with good sense than what is learned in business schools. It is a must read for anyone who wishes to manage effectively.

Dr David James
Senior reporter, *Business Review Weekly* magazine
and author of *Managing for the Twenty First Century*

THE
6-HOUR
MBA

LOUIS A COUTTS

Published by Brolga Publishing Pty Ltd
PO Box 12544 A'Beckett St Melbourne Australia 8006
ABN 46 063 962 443
email: sales@brolgapublishing.com.au
web: www.brolgapublishing.com.au

Graphs on pp. 239 and 240 are used with permission from the publisher, MIT
Center for Advanced Engineering Study, Cambridge, MA 02139.

All efforts have been made to contact the copyright owners of images and any
omissions will be corrected in future reprints.

National Library of Australia Cataloguing-in-Publication entry:

Coutts, Louis A.
The 6-hour MBA
9781921596834 (pbk.)
Management.
Leadership.
658.4

Printed in China
Cover design by David Khan
Typeset by Imogen Stubbs

CONTENTS

Acknowledgements.. VII

Preface...XI

1. Introduction 1

2. Cash 11

3. The concept of exchange 17

4. The concept of benefits................................27

5. Accounting traps...39

6. The theory of the organization 55

7. A short detour in physics.............................75

8. A Case study: Boeing 81

9. Marketing..95

10. Marketing II...105

11. The history of marketing............................. 113

12. Scarcity and Abundance............................ 127

13. Management Accounting I 143

14. Management Accounting II 159

15. Leadership 169

16. Leadership II 191

17. Debt... 197

18. Debtors..209

19. Depreciation 215

20. Change...221

21. Deming 235

22. Epilogue 253

Index...257

ACKNOWLEDGEMENTS

The people who have input into this book and who have
provided me with support in the process of understanding
the concept of the societal nature of corporations are far
too many to be mentioned individually. However, by far
the greatest number of people who have had input are those
thousands of people in the work place who have shared
an hour or so of their lives with me and who have introduced me to the difficulties of people in the workplace in
achieving recognition and self-fulfilment. In a real sense,
this book is for them.

My wife has been an extraordinary force in my work
in management. Having shifted abruptly from law to management, it would have been understandable for her to be
concerned at this career move. In fact, she has supported me
through thick and thin in this journey. She has been a constant and reliable sounding board for my ideas. She has set
bench marks for intellectual rigour and personal behaviour
that have been my light at the end of the tunnel, although,
I am still far from that light.

Professor John Whitney of Colombia University was

my first teacher in management and introduced me to the works of W Edwards Deming who was John's teacher and friend. The influence of John Whitney has been profound and I still use the notes taken in his lectures after more than twenty years. Professor Sunil Erevelles of Belk School of Management, University of North Carolina introduced me to an enormous body of knowledge in the field of management when he was at the Anderson School of Management, UCR. The person who became his wife, undertook research for me that enabled me to explore in depth the detailed world of the human side of enterprise.

Professor Rob Widing who is now Dean of the Macquarie Graduate School of Management has been my mentor in management since we met some fifteen years ago. He has been a regular sounding board for me as a practitioner and has enriched my knowledge and experience of management while becoming a wonderful friend.

Professor Mohan Reddy Dean of the Weatherhead School of Management at Case Western Reserve has a unique mind and I am privileged to be the recipient of his wisdom. It was his encouragement that inspired me to seek publication.

To Professor Dale Davidson and Thunderbird School of Global Management I am eternally grateful. Without their invitation for me to be a visiting Fellow at that great institution and without the resources that they unreservedly provided, I would never have been able to write this book.

To Professor's Morse (Associate Dean, Rochester Institute of Technology) and Hartgraves (Professor Emeritus, Goizueta Business School, Emory University, Atlanta GA), the authors of *Management Accounting*, to which reference is made in the chapters in this book on the subject, I am deeply indebted to them for permitting me to draw on their work. The terminology used by them and some of the examples are so apposite to the theme of this book that it would have been impossible to use better examples.

For some years my son Dr Brendan Coutts worked long and hard to establish the Hawthorne Academy and in doing so, undertook extensive research into the principles that emerge from the Hawthorne studies. In that process, he introduced me to concepts that had escaped me and which form the bone and sinew of this book. Without his enormous contribution, I am certain that my journey in management would have been different and less meaningful than it has been.

During the period of bringing this book to publication I had a health set back which threatened its completion. In that process the support that I received from my doctor, Brian Hassett was beyond any traditional concept of patient dedication. His help and support through some really tough times defies gratitude. In that process, I must also mention my Chinese doctor of Chinese medicine, Dr Qian Wei Wei. I am sure that without her ministrations, I would never have completed this book.

PREFACE

The origins of this book are diverse but there is one particular incident that set me on my management journey. I was a litigation lawyer, confronted with the problem of document production which consumed enormous resources. IBM introduced the first word processor called a magnetic card typewriter. It was frightfully expensive but I was convinced that it was the answer to the stress of document production in my office. I purchased one of the machines and sent my secretary to IBM for a week's course. On the Monday morning after her return from IBM I gave Kaye a series of projects. Later in the morning, I went into her office expecting a miracle only to find Kaye in tears. She was so upset that I had spent so much money but her first experience with the new technology was a disaster.

It was a moment where instinct rather than logic serendipitously played its part. For some reason, I said to Kaye "Don't worry about it. Just go back to your typewriter and when you get a chance, play around with the new technology and we will see how things go". Things went brilliantly and within a week, the technology surpassed my most optimistic expectations. However, I realised that technology was only a mechanistic tool in the hands of people and that people make the difference. Within a year, Kaye had made me an international guru on technology and the law. However, it was that experience of Kaye's tears, caused by my insensitive expectations that has had an enduring influence on my life and firstly influenced me to abandon law and pursue management but more importantly, to constantly have in mind, what has become known as "The human side of enterprise".

Since then, I have had the great good fortune to engage with thousands of people in the workplace, who, in the course of private confidential conversations, have shared a part of their life with me, often revealing some of their most intimate frustrations. I would have to say that statistically, by far the majority of these decent people have been frustrated in their work and their frustration , more often than not, has been a product of insensitive and misguided management.

Over the years, the aggregate of these stories influenced me to investigate the fundamental drivers of successful business because I was convinced that certainly in Western institutions, there is a huge resource in human ingenuity and passion that is not being utilised. One ponders the loss that is inflicted upon our economy as a result of this phenomenon.

In my research as well as in my practice as a management consultant, I realised that despite the emergence of business schools, and the recognition by many academics as to the relationship between human fulfilment and business success, the phenomenon of frustration and mismanagement was profound. The global financial crisis brought home to me the power of misguided management.

A number of themes emerged in this journey and four in particular attracted my attention.

The first was the preoccupation in Western institutions with hierarchy and an expectation that people higher in a hierarchy had authority which should be blindly followed by those lower in the hierarchy.

The second is an assumption that financial incentives are the central and principal motivating influence in productivity.

The third is that the fundamental function of a business is to enhance shareholder value.

These are the current dynamics of modern corporations and I believe them to be profoundly flawed.

The fourth theme that emerged from my conversations was that many people at all levels in organizations had a serious interest in management but believed that to enhance their knowledge it would be necessary to undertake an MBA.

I believed that if we could identify some fundamental drivers of sustainable organizations, it would be possible for management to redirect its focus on the individual as part of a societal entity rather than a mechanistic entity that has as its sole motivation, the enhancement of shareholder value.

I then came across the work of a famous physicist, Richard Feynman, who was a Professor of Physics at CALTEC and a Nobel laureate. He identified that there were some basic concepts in physics that were fundamental to understanding that difficult subject. He conducted a series of six lectures for students who were commencing physics and he reduced these lectures to chapters in a book he called *Six Easy Pieces*.

I wondered whether we could do something similar in

the field of management. I put together a series of lectures and presented them to a group of executives at a conference in Vancouver and received such an encouraging response that I accepted an invitation to be a visiting Fellow at Thunderbird School of Global Management in Phoenix, Arizona to pursue this enterprise.

The result was a series of papers on fundamental and enduring concepts of management that form the chapters of this book.

Hopefully, these thoughts resonate with those thousands of people who have shared precious moments of their lives with me when they have expressed their frustrations in the workplace. Hopefully, I have reduced these concepts to a level of simplicity that they can be understood by many people throughout the workplace so that the knowledge of management will not be seen as some mysterious process understood by a precious few, but a relatively simple discipline that can be embraced by the many. The more people who understand these basic concepts of management, the more likely it is that communication within the workplace will be more meaningful as will the lives of people involved in the human enterprise

Businesses, not for profit entities and governmental utilities are all social beings and they are successful to the extent that the humanity of individuals making up these social entities achieve self-fulfilment and recognition. It is the art of successful living to make a difference and there are few people on this planet who do not possess the desire to do so. Sometimes, management prevents people from attaining this ambition with the result that the organization and the individual suffers. This book is written in the hopes that these inglorious moments that damage the self-esteem of individuals will become fewer and fewer.

INTRODUCTION

Ptolemy was a Greek intellectual who lived between 90 and 168 AD and, while working in Egypt, he became recognised as an expert in many things including astronomy and astrology.

There had long been debate about the status of the earth and its relationship with the universe and particularly the sun. As early as 230 BC, another Greek by the name of Aristarchus came to the conclusion that the earth revolved around the sun. However, homo sapiens, well aware of the emerging importance of the human race could not come to grips with the fact that the Gods had evicted the human race to a minor role in the mystery of the universe. Accordingly, it became more and more popular, without any supporting evidence, to come to the conclusion that because of the pre-eminence of man (which was the term they used in those days) it was inconceivable that the earth was not the centre of the Universe.

Ptolemy was ideally suited to investigate this phenomenon, being installed in a unique establishment in Alexandria in Egypt where he was expected to shed his genius to the world and so he did in many ways. One in particular was to rely on astronomical observations that unequivocally convinced him that the earth was the centre of the Universe and that the planets and the sun formed part of a membrane that circled the earth. He spent many hours of his life coming up with a mathematical explanation for this phenomenon using circles and epicycles turning in their manifold directions, thus complying with observations as to the positions of the planets, stars and sun.

And so Ptolemy's earth centric theory became the accepted wisdom until the fifteenth century when a monk by the name of Copernicus, who undertook rigorous observations of the heavens, came to doubt Ptolemy. By then the hierarchy of the Church had taken hold of the thought processes of the human condition and central to the Church's teaching was the Ptolemaic theory of the universe, despite the fact that Ptolemy had never been a fellow traveller of the Church.

For fifteen hundred years the belief persisted that the earth was the centre of the universe. This belief became entrenched in the dogma of the Church to the extent that Galileo, who used a telescope to survey the heavens and who realised that this earth centric theory was rubbish, had to recant his beliefs in the face of the threat of torture and execution[1]. Gradually science prevailed, but it took the better part of sixteen hundred years for people to come to grips with the fact that our tiny planet is insignificant in the hierarchy of the universe and we are less than a blimp in

---

1   There would appear to be no doubt that Galileo was in real danger with the Church but whether this was because of his beliefs or his arrogant attitude to Church authorities is an issue explored brilliantly by Arthur Koestler in *The Sleep Walkers*.

this incomprehensibly enormous space in which we live.

This is how myths can distort reality and direct people down paths to dead ends. This phenomenon has its current iteration in the never ending emergence of the current snake oil for successful management such as "Quality Assurance and ISO conformity"; "Empowerment"; "Diversity"; "360 degree"; "Performance appraisals" etc. There is absolutely no evidence that any of these wonderful concepts achieve any measurable success across the market place. Indeed, there is evidence that in many cases, their adoption, in the mistaken belief that they are the salvation of a business, actually cause more damage than good.

One myth that did come into existence in the first decade of the last century as a result of the work of an engineer by the name of Frederick Winslow Taylor was that of "scientific management". Despite protestations to the contrary, Taylorism is alive and well today in that employees of organizations are too often looked upon as mechanisms for achieving KPI's. Taylorism, as it has come to be called, was the forerunner of the managerial method of deploying people as "Human Resources" to achieve the objectives of management. This, despite the discovery as early as 1930 that people in the work place were primarily motivated by societal and emotional phenomena and that material or mechanistic paradigms had little influence on productivity. And yet corporations still persist with this concept of people as disposable when not wanted and reusable when they are. This may well be called the Ptolemaic principle at work in the field of management and it pulls in suckers year after year while the fundamental reason for human existence is ignored.

Some corporations see through this nonsense and are doing well but the devastation of the 2008 financial crisis saw a re-emergence of this undying belief in a flawed managerial philosophy. In twenty-four months in the USA there were approximately 54,000 massive layoffs of nearly six million people[2] which doesn't include the smaller lay-offs of small businesses across the country. As a result, the American consumers went on strike and with the downturn of America consumption; the economy went into a tailspin. All because of a Ptolemaic myth that the function of the corporation is to enhance shareholder value at whatever cost; even at the cost of cutting one's own throat.

And so myths become public doctrine and continue to influence people down these cul-de-sacs of history.

What has this got to do with management today?

Myths continue to fill pages of management literature as well as the workplace. There is still persistence in perpetu-ating myths. In this context, and from many years of being in the "cockpits" of distressed companies successfully turn-ing them around, I suspect that the material originating from Business Schools around the world should be subject to much greater circumspection and scrutiny.

Recently I was walking past a class room at a major management school and the lecturer had the serious atten-tion of the students as he was passionately explaining the various theories of pricing. This stuff was straight out of textbooks written by academics who are very smart people but have never sat in the cockpit. I felt like walking into the room and yelling "STOP FOR HEAVEN'S SAKE STOP" because there is now only one theory of pricing and that

---

2   American Bureau of Statistics.

is how to produce goods and services for customers at a cost less than your competitor so that you can meet market prices while improving quality. Businesses can no longer control prices. The world has changed and businesses have to find new ways of bringing products and services to the market with ever-increasing quality and at ever-reducing prices.

The law of price elasticity no longer has general application and indeed, its application only relates to diminishing resources such as oil and even that is doubtful.

The ancient so-called law of supply and demand, based as it was on an assumption of scarcity of supply in the face of abundant demand, is flawed and yet business schools still cling to it as the mantra because Adam Smith discovered it over two centuries ago. Adam Smith was brilliant and one of the great economic thinkers, but he did not envisage the onslaught of technology, competition nor the internet that has educated even the least-astute shopper.

All of the assumptions that have formed the basis of the modern corporation are now under scrutiny and many of them are being found wanting in much the same way as the Ptolemaic theory of the Universe failed to withstand rigorous scientific investigation.

In all of this, one of the worst legacies of ancient times still pervades the business environment and it is the legacy of hierarchy anchored in the ageless culture that perceived some to deserve privilege and some to serve. This cultural phenomenon is directly associated with another myth that the principle purpose of the corporation is to enhance shareholder value.

No matter how enlightened we say we are as a people,

the fact remains that the majority of the people in the workforce today are considered instruments of managerial strategy rather than resources rich with knowledge and experience that could be invaluable to the corporation. There will be many who dispute this, but after conducting thousands of interviews in the work place over the past quarter of a century, it is depressing to consistently come across the invariable story that "I know when I have done something wrong because I get a kick in the behind, but no one ever tells me when I am doing something right. The fact that I don't get a kick in the behind every day suggests that I must be doing something right". How terrible for the human condition to descend to this, when each human person has aspirations to have their own place in the sun.

Another consistent complaint is that "there is no communication in this place. We learn what has been decided once we are told that we have to do something different to what we have been doing".

Sadly, so many people tell me the story of their frustration to the point that they go home at night and want to tell their husband, wife, mother, father, brother, sister or friend about their problems and are met with the response "don't tell me about your problems, I have enough of my own."

Corporations and government instrumentalities are strewn with incompetent management who bring about frustration, loss of production and the inability to access ideas from people who are a rich source of information. That is not to say that all corporations and government bodies are incompetently managed, but the persistence of the stories of frustration, irrespective of the industry, is so consistent as to be compelling evidence that management is not living up to the expectations of people in the twenty-first century.

Despite the proliferation of Business Schools, we are still experiencing shock waves in our economies; huge defaults due to dishonesty; massive unemployment and dislocation of communities; serious dependency upon diminishing resources such as oil without any substantial plan "B"; an American economy that is increasingly dependent upon external borrowings with debt levels in the trillions and a mood across the Northern Hemishperic Western Countries of sobriety in the face of massive unemployment and industrial under utilisation.

Despite this, there is emerging a new style of corporation based on a business model that rejects the traditional concept of the law of supply and demand and increasingly seeks the ability to create an abundance of supply so that there will be an abundance of demand. In 2009 Google chalked up $6.5 billion profits on revenue of $24 billion and the corporation only came into existence in 1998. There is a tendency for these corporations to be associated with a wider justification for existence that involves the recognition of societal needs and the worth of the individual.

While at present, the traditional theories of markets and pricing prevail at Business Schools and major corporations; theories inextricably involved with the concept of shareholder value, there are more and more companies that understand the theory of abundance. These will be the corporations to succeed in the next ten years.

I believe we will see a profound change in the commercial landscape in the next ten years in the form of severe competition with increasing quality and service associated with decreasing prices in a wide variety of industries.

We are entering a period where the only businesses that survive will be those that discover the new paradigm that creating an abundance of supply of quality will lower costs to levels unprecedented. This, after all is the twenty first century.

There are some enduring concepts of management and finance that enable organizations to achieve a sustainable life. In the following chapters I want to introduce these concepts to people across the hierarchy of the work place so that perhaps they can come together in a greater spirit of equilibrium and together, irrespective of their place in the hierarchy of the business, reach a common understanding of these enduring and compelling principles.

Some are more difficult to grasp than others, particularly the chapter in relation to the theory of the corporation, but that section introduces seminal material that has been over-looked or grotesquely misunderstood[3] by modern academia and relates to the fundamental drivers of worker motivation. One finding that has been a constant in subsequent investigations is that there is no evidence that money is a significant motivator of people in the workplace. And yet, it is still the carrot of the Ptolemy's of management today.

There is a fundamental truism and that is the innate

---

3   For many years, folklore has grown up about the Hawthorne experiments which were conducted between 1928 and 1933 in a factory in Chicago. These experiments are now believed by many to relate to the measurement of productivity in the factory according to the extent to which lighting was increased and decreased. In fact, the experiments had nothing to do with lighting. The experiments, of which there were eleven, are documented in a detailed book published by Harvard (Dixon & Roethlisberger, *Management and the Worker*, HUP, 1939) and written by those who conducted the experiments, had nothing to do with lighting but a lot to do with the human factors that influence workers.

decency of most people and their desire to do their best and achieve a certain place in the sun. Somehow we recognise that but when the chips are down and the next quarter's numbers are on the line, we make terrible mistakes. I know because I am just as guilty as many others.

CASH

You can read all sorts of stuff about business, learn about the latest snake oil approach to riches and get two MBA's while establishing yourself as an expert to whom people turn for advice, but if you don't understand the nature and importance of cash in a business, you will soon rue your ignorance.

There are few more disturbing experiences in the life of a turnaround professional to walk back into a business after just paying a visit to the business's bank where you have been told by the bank manager that she is going to bounce the next pay cheques. As you walk in and see all of these lovely people working away, totally unaware of the catastrophe that is about to fall on them, a range of emotions flow through the body and mind. An emotion of anger at the managers who have brought about this state of affairs; an emotion of sympathy for these innocent victims of incompetence and an emotion of wonder that such a basic concept of cash is not understood. Often, banks are complicit in this devastating scenario. In the end, emotions don't solve problems but rather interfere with cool, clinical diagnosis, and that is what you want when the money runs out.

The lack of cash in any business is a symptom of something more fundamentally wrong. When management understands the concept of cash it is more likely to avoid shortages and thus to avoid the cover up for ignorance by resorting to the oft quoted explanation "we just have a cash flow problem at the moment".

In the chapter on accounting we will talk in detail about the cash business cycle and how it works. By way of introduction, the concept is simple. Once a business goes through a cycle of acquiring the necessities for delivering benefits to customers, be those benefits in the way of goods or services, there should be more money in the bank at the end of the cycle than at the beginning; otherwise there is no point in being in business.

In the case of a wholesale entity, there is the process of acquiring goods or bringing them into existence by way of manufacture and on selling them to a third party that may be a retailer. Once the sale to the retailer is complete, there should be more money in the bank account of the wholesaler or manufacturer than beforehand.

In the case of a service provider such as an insurance company, lawyer or doctor, there should be more money in the bank once the service is delivered than beforehand.

This of course is a simplification as most businesses have manifold sales. As a result we take a wider timeframe and say that there should be more money in the bank at the end of a year than there was at the beginning. This is a simple test as to whether or not a business is successful. It is important to remember that we are talking about cash, and as we shall see, sometimes management confuses profit with cash. Cash is something in the bank that can be spent. Profit is something on the books that is not necessarily cash. It is the health of the bank balance that determines the ability of a business to continue to trade.

This brings me back to that sickly scenario of walking into a business after visiting the bank with the knowledge that these people's jobs are in jeopardy, as are their wages. The cash business cycle has been going backwards, which means that the business has been doing something wrong. It is not a cash problem, but rather a management problem.

Sometimes a business can have great assets like real estate but no cash income. There is often a tendency on the part of management to borrow against the asset while the cost of operations continues. All that happens in this scenario is that the debt increases and the equity in the asset decreases.

As long as the cash of the business is declining or the business is going into increasing debt, the business is at risk; with the result that management often get early warning signs if they are alert to this trend. However, there is a tendency for managers to convince themselves that the negative cash flow is temporary and a bit of borrowing will get them by until things turn up.

Time was against me when I walked back into the business after receiving the message from the bank that it was going to bounce the pay cheque. Management was desperate to borrow more money, but I knew that without some strategy to turn the ship around, even if it was possible to borrow more money, the additional borrowings would simply result in a bigger hole from which it would be impossible to emerge.

As I looked at these people, who I am sure were aware that things weren't going well but were unaware of how bad they were, I knew that collectively they shared the story of the organization and so they almost certainly knew the solution. After all, people are the business. In the chain of suppliers, employees and customers, there is this wider story of the business that properly ascertained, will throw the most accurate and penetrating light on its strengths and weaknesses. When the business is going south, these are the only people who can help and so it was that I turned to them to quickly get the story of the business. I had a few days and was able to conduct a whole series of one-on-one confidential interviews, until gradually the entire story of mismanagement and reckless application of funds emerged.

One of many issues that arose was the extent to which management was using the firm's finances for their personal use; cars, houses, horses, yachts, holidays and on and on. These adventures were all using up the cash resources of the firm and by the time I had identified them, taken them out of the finances of the business and told management that they had to pick up the cheque for them, we could go back to the bank and establish that the firm could provide a positive cash flow.

That gave us a bit of time in which to identify the consequences of the neglect of management of the affairs of the business while pursuing these grandiloquent pastimes that were sending the firm bankrupt. Gradually, a healthy cash business cycle re-emerged and in the process management learnt the meaning of staying close to its people so as not to get off the rails in the future. Management also learnt the preciousness of cash flowing from operations rather than borrowings.

If management had woken up earlier to the fact that the disappearance of positive cash flow was a symptom rather than something to be addressed by simply borrowing more money, all the pain that they had to undergo would have been avoided. However, they learnt the great lesson of the relationship between the potential of people in the organisation, the necessity to meet customer satisfaction and cash flow.

THE CONCEPT OF EXCHANGE

Clarence Saunders worked as a salesman for a wholesale grocer back at the turn of the last century and had previously worked in a grocer's shop, having left school at the age of fourteen. In those days, the typical grocer stood behind the counter of the store with the stock on the shelves at the rear of the shop. People would have to line up to be served and point to the items on the shelves that they wanted. These goods frequently were unwrapped and the person behind the counter would have to weigh whatever was ordered, such as sugar or flour, put it in a bag and then hand it to the customer and request payment. Often the customer, who lived just around the corner would ask the grocer to put it "on the slate" which was the way one asked for credit. They would have to frequent the grocer, because in those days, most people didn't have a car and there was a limit to how much they could carry.

Saunders thought this was an inefficient and costly way of providing a service and it is said that he put to his boss the idea of starting a self-service grocery. That didn't appeal to the boss all that much and so he was either fired or left and started his own super market in 1916 in Memphis Tennessee[1]. It addressed many of the concerns that he believed customers of the traditional grocery store experienced. Customers didn't have to wait to be served, they could directly go to the shelves and select the individual groceries themselves, they had a wider collection of products and the prices were cheaper. Saunders actually patented his ideas and called his store Piggly Wiggly. The idea took on and Saunders franchised an increasing number of stores. By 1923, his industry disruptive idea caught the attention of some big boys on Wall St who couldn't comprehend that an upstart like Saunders could change the grocery industry.

The big boys engaged a guy called Merrill (of Merrill Lynch fame) to drive down the price of Piggly Wiggly stock so that it could either be acquired for a song or send Saunders bankrupt. So, these guys started to "sell" stock that they didn't own. In fact, they were selling it in bucketfulls until 196,000 of the 200,000 shares on issue were in fact "sold". What these big boys didn't know was that Saunders was the buyer of the stock. It is rumoured that he took a train to New York with a million dollars in cash in order to trump these gangsters (has anything changed?) So, when he insisted on delivery of the shares that the "sellers" were selling, they didn't have them which meant, in ordinary circumstances, they would have to actually go to the market and buy them. But who owned them? Saunders had appeared to call these guys' bluff and was sitting waiting for them to deliver the share certificates. In those days it was necessary to deliver share certificates within twenty four

---

1   At that stage, the "T" model Ford was making the ownership of a motor vehicle affordable to many who previously could not afford a car.

hours of purchase. Saunders was sitting pretty. However, he was an outsider.

Saunders had borrowed heavily to make his play on the market. However, behind the scenes, the rules suddenly altered. The stock exchange changed the rules so that the gangsters, who were shafting Saunders, were allowed five days to deliver the stock instead of the usual twenty four hours. In the meantime, miraculously, the bank that had lent the money to Saunders insisted on repayment immediately. As usual, Wall St came out on top and Saunders went bankrupt but Piggly Wiggly stores continued to thrive in the hands of the whiz kids of Wall St and were ultimately merged into a company that ended up with the name "Safeway".

Anyway, sorry for what might appear to be a detour but its relevance will become clearer later in this chapter. Let us go back. Why was Saunder's idea so successful? The answer is that while the groceries purchased by the customers were needed by the customer, the process of acquiring them was often an irritant. America in those days was on the verge of what might be called "the coin in the slot" era where more and more frequently people who decided that they wanted something wanted it NOW! As the motor vehicle developed and people could carry more goods in one shopping, they could go to the super market and get everything they wanted and at less frequent intervals than in the old days when they went to the grocer's shop.

The idea was brilliant because it not only gave people options but it also conferred a number of incredibly important benefits on them. They didn't have to queue up to shop (mind you, today, getting caught behind six people at the checkout who are purchasing the next six months rations is quite an experience); they could select their own goods in their own time; they had a choice: the price was lower than the old grocery store and with the automobile they could purchase all that they needed for a longer period. It wasn't the novelty of the idea that drove people from the grocery store to the supermarket. They defected to this new idea because of the manifold benefits that they perceived to be involved.

What was in it for Saunders? For a start, people paid cash at the checkout. They didn't mind that because they were getting the stuff cheaper than they did at the corner store. In addition, he was getting turn over far greater than the local grocer, which meant of course he could reduce his margins and at the same time make more money.

Saunders had an idea that made people other than him enormously wealthy because his motivation in developing the idea was to bring a benefit to people that currently did not exist in the market place. The proof of his idea is now in the pudding.

• • •

By the fifteenth century The Roman Catholic Church was the dominant institution throughout Europe and England and held the vast majority of the inhabitants in its theological grasp. Its anchor and authority was contained in a document called the *Bible*, which it was fond of quoting but often guilty of ignoring. Around about 1444 there was some evidence that a guy called Gutenberg had developed the idea of building a printing press. It is said that it was used to print indulgences that the salespeople claimed liberated the purchaser of the indulgence from the severity of eternal punishment and the early release after death from purgatory to heaven.

Anyway, Gutenberg came up with the idea that if he could print the bible, he would have a huge market. All of those people who had had the bible quoted to them all their life would surely want to buy it if it could be produced en masse. In this he was right but his problem was money. Guttenberg was a poor business man and decided to fund his enterprise with debt. Accordingly, he entered into an agreement with a "friend" who was a money lender by the name of Johan Fust whereby Fust agreed to lend Gutenberg the money to complete this incredible enterprise. However, some days before the first print run of Guttenberg's Bible, Fust decided that Gutenberg was squandering his money and so he went to Court and had Gutenberg bankrupted and obtained an order transferring the press and the bible printing to him. Fust, who had been wealthy beforehand, ended up with an asset that made him enormously wealthy while, Gutenberg ended up with the backside out of his pants.

Here was a guy who saw a need in the market. What would the availability of the bible do to the masses of people who hitherto had to rely on the words of churchmen (many of whom had doubtful motives)? They could have a look at the bible itself and see what it really said. The benefit that it conferred and is still conferring on the masses of people around the world is incomprehensible. It also had something to do with the emergence of the questioning of the profligacy of those who had hitherto hidden behind the words of that invisible book of authority.

• • •

Anyway, these stories are by way of introduction to understanding the basic concept of a sustainable business. There are six main lessons:

1. Unless a business consistently delivers to its customers benefits that the customer consider to be of value to them, and particularly a value that is worth more to them than the price, that business will not survive.

2. Unless the business also gets benefits equal to or greater than the value of the benefits it is conferring on a customer, it will not survive;

3. Unless your bankroll is sufficient to see you through, the business will not survive;

4. If a business does not understand the function of money (cash), it won't survive (or if it does, it will be a fluke);

5. If people running the business do not build strong bonds of trust with the people involved in the business it will find the going tough and won't be as successful as those businesses that do have this level of trust;

6. If you float on the stock exchange, you have to learn to swim with the sharks.

You might have detected here that I have not mentioned the words product or price which are two of the famous four P's of marketing. No, I am not breaking new ground or talking nonsense because one of the leading text books[2] on marketing actually goes to great lengths to make the point that business is about exchanging benefits. Let's see what it says:

2　P Kotler, *Marketing Management,* 9th edn, Prentice Hall 1997, p. 11.

"whether exchange takes place depends upon whether the two parties can agree on terms of exchange that will leave them both better off (or at least not worse off) than they were before the exchange.

Exchange is frequently described as a value creating process because exchange normally leaves both parties better off."

This is the concept of exchange which is older than the hills being the principle of commerce before the invention of currency. That early principle of commerce is now called "bartering" although I am not sure what it was called back in the days of the cave men.

Even if you don't get around to reading Kottler or you never read a book on marketing or business, if you are interested in a business being sustainable, burn the quotation into your mind and use it as a guiding principle until you come across a better one.

You might note that in introducing the five important elements of a business I used the word "sustainable". Businesses come and go and in the words of a famous commentator on sustainable business[3], "Survival is not compulsory". What is compulsory if a business is to be sustainable over the long haul is that both the vendor (the business) and the customer have to consistently go away from transactions with one another feeling that they have each got a great deal. At the same time, the great deal so far as the business is concerned is that it is making sufficient money to continue to enhance the benefits so that it can

---

3   W Edwards Deming, *Out of the Crisis,* 18th edn, CUP, 1992.

stay in business and grow.

This is a pretty simple formula, but in this twenty-first century where price, quality and service are the drivers of competitive advantage, there are a few tricks that we need to know about in managing our business from day-to-day with the vision that the business will still be successful in years to come. In fact, there are many tricks and a lot of people learn them along the way without going to business schools[4], but while there are many tools that can be used in managing businesses, from time to time it is important to concentrate on some principles because every now and then there is the need for new tools and it is impossible to identify the tools that are necessary without understanding the principles that draw all these different threads together.

This is a book about some of the basic principles of management, which I believe are enduring and, as I indicated earlier, the concept of exchange is as old as the cave men.

In Chapter 6 I will look at this issue of trust that is number five in the issues mentioned earlier in this chapter, because without trust running through the process of commerce, we can forget sustainability.

Almost all businesses are what we call "organizations". As Adam Smith pointed out towards the end of the eighteenth century, with the advent of the industrial revolution it was discovered that an organization bringing together a number of people could achieve more than could be achieved by individuals alone. Since then, the organization has been the backbone of our industrial society. Accordingly, it is necessary to understand the nature of organizations and

---

4   Bill Gates quit Stanford before graduating.

how they work[5].

For the moment, let us get back to the fundamental drivers of exchange which are the benefits conferred on and enjoyed by the parties to the exchange, these parties being the vendor and the purchaser

---

5   There are many so called "one person" businesses and I conducted one for quite some years. However, that entity is still an organization of many because it embraces a range of stakeholders who become intimate with the business including suppliers and customers, not to mention the manifold moods and personalities of the owner.

THE CONCEPT
OF BENEFITS

One way of expressing the function of an organization is to say that its purpose is to bring about an exchange of benefits that the organization and its various stake holders such as suppliers, employees and customers, perceive to be equal to or greater than the benefits offered in return. In facilitating these various exchanges, the organization achieves profits that ensure its sustainability.

Instead of defining the function of a corporation in terms of enhancing shareholder value, let us see if there is a more appropriate description of its function. The fundamental function of an organization is to bring about an exchange of benefits that are perceived by its suppliers, employees and customers to equal or exceed the benefits offered in return. In facilitating these exchanges, the organization achieves profitability that ensures sustainable shareholder value. It might be worth adding that to the extent to which the benefits conferred by an organization on its customers have societal merit, its ongoing sustainability and hence share-holder value are more likely to be enhanced.

In this context the concept of benefits emerges as significant and it is proper to dwell a little in understanding more clearly the term "benefit".

In the traditional concept of a business there is a great emphasis on the necessity to make a profit and of course[1] it is essential for businesses to make a profit otherwise they fold unless they are too big to fail like a General Motors or a Merrill Lynch. But those ordinary mortals that go about their business from day to day, dealing as best they can with the vagaries of the economy and the unpredictability of the bureaucracy, simply have to make a profit to survive. As we will see in a later discussion, it is not only necessary to make a profit but more specifically to make a cash profit. The difference between the two statements will soon emerge quite clearly. However, in the context of the exchange theory of management, the principle purpose of the business is to create value in an exchange and thereby make a sustainable profit. In one case, profit is the reason to be in business whereas in the other, creating value is the reason to be in business with profit its consequence.

In this traditional approach to management of the organization the basis by which it determines its profit is by a simple formula which I call the "bean counters" formula. It goes something like this:

"How many will I sell at what price and what will it cost?"

If the number of sales multiplied by the price is greater than the cost, the bean counters then ask another question.

---

1   These days there is still a prevailing view that the purpose of the organization is to enhance shareholder value, despite the frequency with which this dominant purpose has wreaked havoc not only within the company but across the financial world.

*"How much will we have to invest
in order to bring about this result?"*

The reason they ask this question is to determine whether the return they will get on their investment meets their expectations. For instance, the company might be able to buy safe Treasury bonds at a yield of 5% without risk. Accordingly if the business is to invest in a product line, it has to satisfy itself that the return it will get on its invest-ment (frequently referred to as the ROI) has to be better than an investment in Treasury bonds and indeed, it has to be a lot better because of the risks involved in bringing a product to the market as against having money with the Treasury.

Sales × Price − Cost = Profit.

Profit divided by capital invested × 100 = % ROI

This is an understandably hard-nosed approach to the use of the funds of the corporation. And these trustees of the shareholder interest have to be pretty damned careful in these calculations not only because the shareholder interest is at stake but often something far more important and that is the performance remuneration of the executive.

In the context of our discussion about the function of the organization, I wonder if there is something missing in this formula. Let us see what is missing. We have to ask the question why someone would pay a price for something that the organization is selling. Now this question starts you thinking. Why would someone buy my product? This is such a simple question and such an obvious one to ask but so often people go into businesses with their ears back and eyes closed without turning their mind to this fundamental issue.

And the answer from the customer's point of view is "because the benefit I, the customer will receive is equal to or greater than the benefit I perceive to be conferring on the vendor". That is only part of the answer because the vendor business will say "because the benefit conferred on me by the customer is equal to or greater than the value I am conferring on the customer" The issue of competitive choices will also influence the decision by the customer.

Just as I suggested in Chapter 2 that you must never forget the definition of exchange quoted in that chapter, so you should never forget that what businesses sell are benefits.

In Melbourne, Australia, there is a world famous tourist site called the Victoria Market. People go there from all over the world. One part of the market is devoted to the sale of fruit and vegetables from dismountable stalls on the bitumen floor of a tin roof covered marketplace. Everything is fresh and cheap. The prices beat the supermarket prices by hundreds of per cent. Not only do tourists flock there but the locals turn up in their thousands. They often travel some distance, and in their shopping, they feel that they would like a snack. It has to be handy to the stalls and be quick and inexpensive. Welcome the donut stall where a few guys park their converted bus on the kerb and make fresh juicy hot donuts on the spot. You can see them making the things. They sell six for five dollars. Just about anywhere else you go for a donut will cost at least a dollar donut, and generally speaking they are not fresh. The donut stall is parked outside the market on the five days a week the market is opened and sells donuts for at least seven hours. There is always a queue. Sometimes it might only be twelve people and other times it might be twenty but you can guarantee that there is always someone waiting in a queue. It takes twelve seconds to hand over six hot donuts in a neat clean paper bag and collect $5. This twelve second exchange occurs throughout the day, five days a week and nearly fifty-two weeks a year.

The people running this donut stall have no illusions about what they are doing. They are making donuts but they are selling benefits. They are cheaper than anyone else; their donuts are better and fresher than anyone else's and they realise that here in the market are a lot of people who want to get their shopping done and go home but want something quick and fresh to eat on the run.

At the same market, there is another little business. This business rents a couple of small strips of bitumen at three different points around the market and covers the site with a tarpaulin. Before I go on I am including pictures of some of the stalls of the market and you will see huge amounts of fruit and vegetables which are as cheap as you can get.

Now, this is not a Clarence Saunders supermarket, although it is generally "help yourself" and people do by the thousands. However, there is a catch that when you seen an abundance of supply at dirt cheap prices, there is a tendency to buy a lot of the stuff. The trouble is you have to carry it all home or to the apartment that tourists are renting. Damm! But rescue is in store because under those tarpaulins are a stack of shopping trolleys that you can rent for $3. There is always a queue of people lining up to pay $3 for the trolley. One site alone houses two hundred and eighty trolleys, and on some days, particularly near

Christmas and during holiday periods, all of those trolleys are out and there is a line waiting.

The woman who runs the show realised there was a serious need not only on the part of visitors to the market but also on the part of the people selling their stuff. Without shopping trolleys, a lot of people would be restricted in what they could buy, but with shopping trolleys they could buy more stuff, the stall operator could sell more stuff and the woman running the trolley business could make money. That woman is not in the business of hiring trolleys and she knows it. She is in the business of bringing benefits to the shoppers and the shopkeepers. The solution to the needs is simple, cheap and effective. Everyone who participates in that arrangement is completely satisfied. The people who pay their three bucks think that they are getting a bargain in relation to the value it creates.

They are simple stories of exchange of benefits that demonstrate the fundamental drivers of sustainable business.

If the owners of those two businesses had simply decided that they wanted to make a lot of money they might have tried their luck on the stock exchange or in the property market. What they realised was that given their skills, they could satisfy a need and in doing so make a profit. They ticked all of the boxes of marketing probably without knowing that the boxes existed. They identified a market segment with a need and a benefit that would satisfy that need. They then worked out a price that would reach the lowest common denominator of customer financial capacity. They also kept an eye on cost by renting a piece of kerb side on cobble stones and making their donuts on site.

Look at the advertisement for Crest toothpaste.

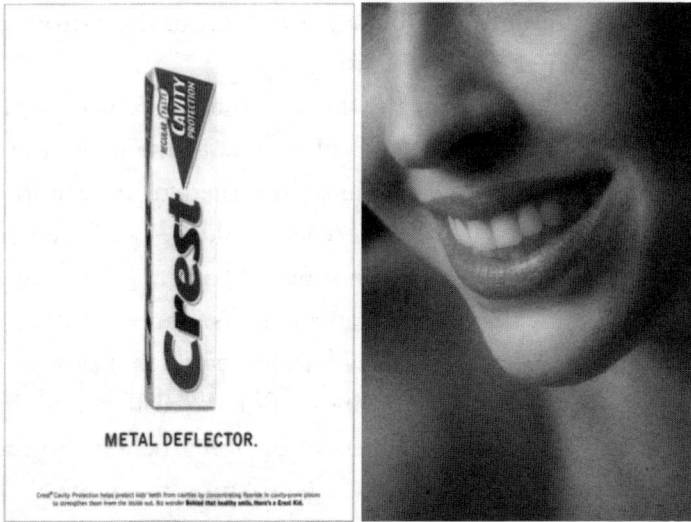

METAL DEFLECTOR.

Crest® Cavity Protection helps protect kids' teeth from cavities by concentrating fluoride in cavity-prone places to strengthen them from the inside out. No wonder **Behind that healthy smile, there's a Crest Kid.**

I can't read the small print but I can't see at a glance the mention of tooth paste. I can see the name Crest on a packet that suggests it is a tooth paste and I can see the photograph of an attractive woman with lovely teeth. What is Crest selling here? "You can have teeth like this if you use our new beaut metal deflector". If that isn't selling a benefit I will ... well.

Let us get away from stories and do some simple algebra. Instead of asking the question "How many will we sell?" let us ask the question "what creates revenue?" Clearly, the answer is that sales drive revenue. So, then we ask "what drives sales?" We know the answer to that:

BENEFITS DRIVE SALES

Let us now rephrase the formula for calculating profit.

The question now becomes "How many benefits will people buy from me?" The answer surely is "It depends upon the price". But someone might ask, "What about quality?" The answer to this question is that quality is a function of price in the context of the sale of benefits. If the quality is poor, the price will have to be low enough to represent value. People use price to gauge the extent of the benefit. If they feel the price is too high, they won't buy because they feel that the deal doesn't represent value. The only people who will buy if they feel that the deal doesn't represent value are people who are captive audiences, and these people generally have long memories and longer tongues. If the price is low it is important to make sure that the benefit being sold still represents value. Once we introduce this ageless concept of benefit into the discussion about business, it is important to remember that no matter what the price, it has to represent value that will induce a sufficient number of people to purchase the benefit and come back again while telling others about the benefit. Otherwise, there is no sustainability in the business.

Following is a diagram of how to measure benefits:

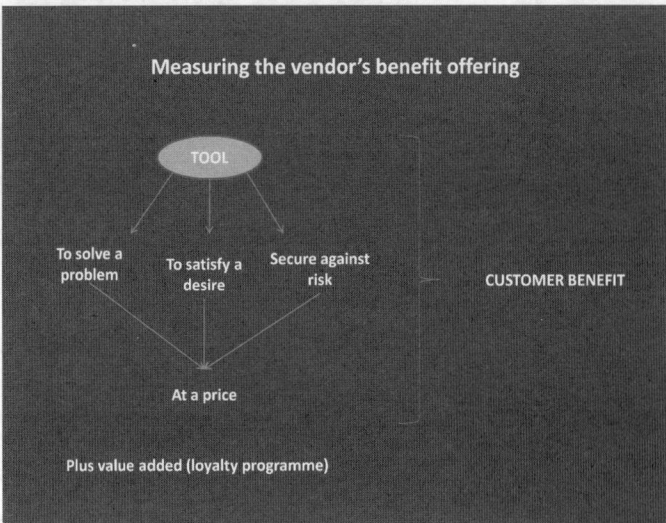

Measuring the vendor's benefit offering

TOOL

To solve a problem

To satisfy a desire

Secure against risk

CUSTOMER BENEFIT

At a price

Plus value added (loyalty programme)

If you substitute the word "tool" for benefits you will see that it serves different people in different ways. For the purpose of this diagram I have chosen three different segments. The first tool is to solve a problem such as helping me carry a lot of produce to my car from the market. The second type of tool is to satisfy a desire such as being entertained at the theatre. The third type of tool is security against risk like an insurance policy or a stop loss order on the stock exchange. All of these tools have a price and end up conferring a customer benefit. This represents the "vendor offering".

What does the customer offer in return? Have a look at the following diagram.

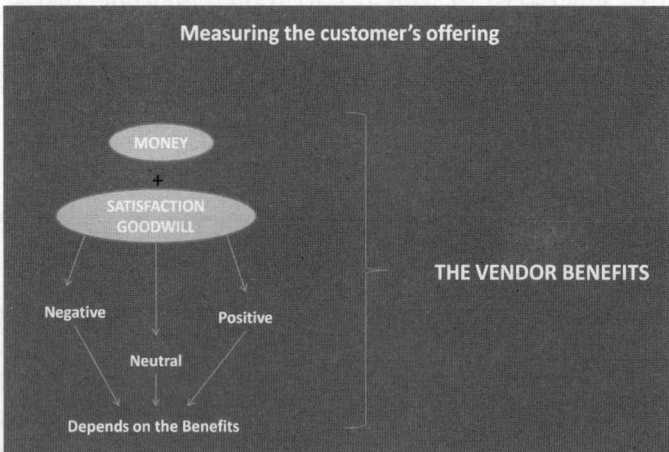

The first thing that the customer offers the vendor is money. Then we enter the important arena of business. Can the customer offer more than money? If the answer is "no", there is no sustainable business. Let's look more closely at the diagram. After the term "money" is a plus sign; after that comes the term "goodwill". Read on and we can see that the goodwill can in fact be negative. Who hasn't ever walked out of a shop because they can't attract the attention of a salesperson or there is in fact no one to help?

The goodwill can be neutral. How can that be? You walk into J C Penney's looking for a pair of gloves. There is a pair on sale so you pick up the gloves and go to the counter and a lovely lady takes your money and gives you the gloves. So, what is the big deal? Do you go racing out of Penney's yelling to the world that you have had a wonderful retail experience? It was neither good nor bad. In such a situation, goodwill is simply neutral. You simply got what you wanted for a price.

But wait because goodwill can be positive.

You go into J C Penney's wanting to buy a pair of gloves and see some on the counter for a quarter of their original price. You pick them up and go to pay with your debit card and the till won't read the stinking card. You get embarrassed because the sign comes back "not approved". Now the woman could have just told me that she couldn't help. Instead, she says "I will try something else" and after a few tries she discovered that the bank hasn't disowned you and it approves the transaction. You then say that you are going to the Grand Canyon and so you don't want her to put the gloves in a bag so instead she cuts off all the tickets etc so that the gloves can be worn straight away. You then see an item on a throw out table which is a child's video recorder for $17. So, you go back to the lady and ask her if she knows anything about them and she says that she does. She says they are fantastic and she purchased one herself for her granddaughter. She then gave a detailed description of what it did (and she is in Men's clothing) and how it worked. You tell a lot of people about this episode at J C Penney's. That is how a simple exchange can turn the goodwill factor from neutral to positive.

The experience in Penney's could have been a straight transaction and you would have walked out happy with the bargain but after all, that happens every day in retail. You wouldn't have thought more about it. You got what you wanted (a great benefit as it turned out in the snow in Northern Arizona) and paid for it. But the experience became just that little more that made you remember so that you will go back to Penney's when you have a need for their products.

All this amounts to the fact that the customer can confer a lot more on a vendor than money. Sometimes positive goodwill means more to a vendor than the price of an individual benefit.

Basically, the formula for growth is that if goodwill is negative, growth will be negative; if neutral there will be no growth. However, if goodwill is positive, the business will grow.

ACCOUNTING TRAPS

Extract from a Birthday Card
Question "Do you want to know how to double
your money?"
Answer "Fold it"

TRAP ONE: ACCRUAL ACCOUNTING

Accounting is a tricky business as many executives have discovered. Just have a look at this graph.

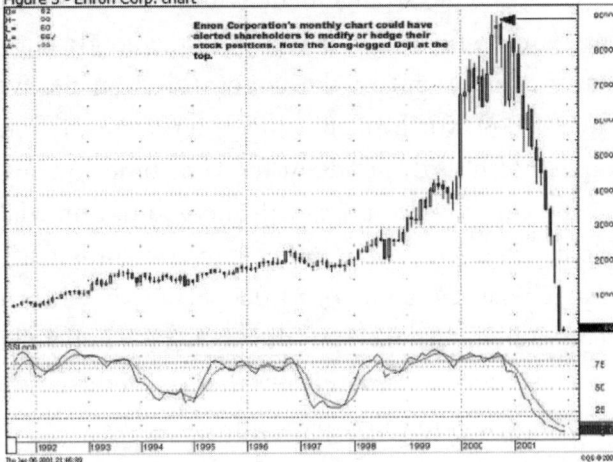

Figure 3 - Enron Corp. chart

Enron Corporation's monthly chart could have alerted shareholders to modify or hedge their stock positions. Note the Long-legged Doji at the top.

In the space of nine years, the Executives of Enron were able to release audited financial statements to the markets that persuaded investors (and some of them were big time) to push the share price from under $30 to $90, only to see that price evaporate in the space of months and senior executives end up in gaol.

Whenever we prepare or look at financial statements, we should have this graph in mind, because to a lesser extent this phenomenon occurs regularly in business. It can happen honestly by following traditional methods of accounting. If that sends a shiver down your spine; great; because it will alert you to one of the great traps of accounting arising out of a technique in common use called "accrual accounting". I am not an accountant and so I am not sure of the origins of accrual accounting but it wouldn't surprise me if it was invented by someone in the Internal Revenue Authority. The reason for this will emerge quite soon.

This is how accrual accounting works. You are in the business of selling sporting goods to retail stores. In other words, you are a wholesaler. Your customers (the retail sports stores) have a credit arrangement with you whereby they don't pay you on the order or receipt of the goods, but only thirty days after receipt of the goods. OK, you receive an order for $1,000 worth of sporting goods from the retailer and you despatch those goods. At the same time you raise an invoice and that invoice goes with the goods. Immediately the invoice goes to the computer which records that you have just generated income of $1,000. Hang on, where's the cash? The cash, my friends is in the pocket (or hopefully so) of your retail customer and remains there until the customer pays you, hopefully in thirty days' time.

In the meantime, you are an honest operator and so you have paid for the goods you have just sold, which means that you are out of pocket for whatever those goods cost you. Let us say you paid $500 for the goods. Now you can see why the tax department is quite interested in accrual accounting because once you have paid for the goods, that amount is recorded in your accounts as expenditure. The moment the cheque is raised, the amount is debited against your income. So, before you have despatched your goods to the retailer, your expenditure shows that you have spent $500 and that is a cost and also a taxation deduction. Then you send out the invoice for $1,000 and that is shown as your income. Bingo, you have made a profit of $500! But where is the cash? Once again, it is in the pocket (or hopefully so) of your customer. If you lodge your tax return immediately after sending out the invoice and before you receive the money, your taxable profit is $500 and you then have to find the money to pay the tax because the $500 profit is not in your pocket. Do, you see how beautiful this scheme is from the point of view of the tax department? The taxation department is not interested in whether or not you have received the money; it only wants you to pay the tax on the notional profit you have received.

In accrual accounting, expenditure (which is cash out) goes out the door immediately but income is taken into account before it is received and at the very moment the invoice is raised.

All of these transactions are recorded in what is called the "Profit and Loss account". In the simplest way of recording this transaction with your sporting good customer the profit and loss account will look something like this:

Revenue	$1,000
Expenditure	$ 500
Profit	$ 500

I come across a lot of people who proudly show me accounts like this to indicate that they are making a great profit. However, they say that the reason the company is in trouble is that it is having "cash flow problems". Whenever you hear that explanation, let another shiver go through your spine because it generally means that the accounts are playing tricks and almost always it has to do with this technique of accrual accounting.

Just suppose you have made the wrong call with your sports good customer and he or she doesn't pay you the $1000 on time. Your income statement still shows that you had income of $1,000 and you have to keep trading by paying your bills and then you have to pay your tax, but you still can't get the stinking $1,000 from your customer. That's when you get a cash flow problem[1]. Now the accounts show that the $1,000 is on your books even though you haven't received it; so where is it?

Another area of accounting that can play tricks is in what is called the balance sheet. The balance sheet merely records the assets and liabilities of the company. Suppose we make the sports wholesaler accounts just a little more complicated. Let us suppose that the wholesaler has borrowed the $500 to purchase the goods it has sold to the retailer but the bor-

---

1   This is only one of many reasons for cash flow problems but I mention it here because it is such a regular occurrence that get people into difficulty that they should be aware of the problem, even though it is obvious.

rowing of that money and the payment of it to the original vendor together with the sale are the only transactions to date in the company. The balance sheet is going to look like this:

ASSETS	
Debtors	$1,000
LIABILITIES	
Debt to bank	$ 500
Net assets	$ 500

While your profit and loss account shows that you have made a profit, the balance sheet indicates that you don't have any money because all of your cash is tied up with the retailer. If the retailer pays the debt of $1,000, your Profit and Loss account won't alter but your balance sheet will because you will bring to account in your balance sheet the $1,000 you receive from the retailer. This will pay off your debt and you will have cash in the bank. Your Balance sheet will then look like this:

ASSETS	
Money in Bank	$500
Liabilities	0
Net assets	$500

TRAP TWO: THE TRICKS OF THE BALANCE SHEET

The balance sheet that we used in the last section seems to look fine. Sure, the retailer owes the money and debts are assets in the hands of businesses who are owed the money. However, something strange happens on occasions and people don't pay their bills. The moment I see debtors in a balance sheet I immediately make inquiries as to how long those debts have been owed. Oh my goodness! Often when I ask this question, no one has ever really looked and what I discover is that money has been owed by some people well outside the trading terms. When I look into it further, there are many explanations for the debtor not paying. Sometimes they simply don't have the money. On other occasions you find that they have been complaining for a long time about the shoddy product and want something done about it, but no one has responded to the request and so the bill goes unpaid. So, you look at the debtors and say to yourself "you are not going to recover all this money; some of it will have to be written off".

At this stage, something quite unnerving happens to the wholesaler because a write off means that you go back to your profit and loss account. Suppose it is only possible to recover $500 of the $1,000 owing, you have to go to the expenditure side of the P & L and insert "bad debt written off" $500. Suddenly, all of the accounts alter and they don't have the pleasant appearance they had when the sale of $1,000 was made

For instance, the Profit and Loss account looks something like this:

Revenue	$1,000
Expenditure	
Purchases	$500
Bad debts written off	$500
Profit	$0

Assuming the remaining $500 is used to pay off the bank loan, the Balance sheet will look like this:

Assets	0
Liabilities	0
Net assets	0

It is amazing how many people in business delude themselves into believing they are doing well when in fact they aren't. And it is not just small businesses that get into these difficulties. Big businesses have mind blowing irregularities and yet present their reports to the markets as though everything is fine. Enron is a case in point.

One of Enron's businesses was to sell contracts for the supply of natural gas to utilities. The contracts might be to supply them with gas at a price in ten years' time or over a period of ten years. Once the contract was signed and no natural gas had been supplied, no money passed hands between the utility and Enron. However, there is an accounting technique, similar to the accrual technique, called "mark to market" which somehow justified Enron's auditors to bring to account in the year the contract was written the projected profit in the contract over the ten year period. Wow! Did that do something to Enron's bottom line and these were the accounts audited by an international accounting firm for all the market to see.

Enron was defying gravity! It had discovered a new way to make money! In fact, all it had done was to discover a way to deceive people into believing that it was making money. The actual cash in relation to these contracts would not be received for years and there was no certainty that when received there would be a profit. In the meantime, Enron had to pay its bills and resorted to all sorts of tricks which effectively consisted of "financial mirrors" until there was no more cash in the tin, and even if the utilities could pay the money in ten years, Enron couldn't last that long because it had run out of cash, and more importantly, the confidence of the market.

Suddenly the castle came tumbling down and a lot of people lost a lot of money and others went to prison and a lot of lawyers made a lot of money all over the traps that can lie behind a balance sheet and a Profit and Loss account.

TRAP THREE: MISREADING THE BALANCE SHEET

I have been constantly amazed at techniques used by executives to keep their businesses going when they don't have a positive cash flow. The first thing they seem to do is to go to the bank and say "we have a cash flow problem". Now, I am not a banker but I know that as soon as someone says something like that, there is trouble brewing because there is no point in being in business unless at the end of the day you have more cash in the bank than at the beginning. The executive then hands over to the bank the perfectly presented financial statements including the Profit and Loss account that indicates the business has a healthy profit and then they hand over the balance sheet that shows that the business has net assets. But one of the assets of course is the amount of money owed to the company by its customers In Balance Sheet terms, we call this amount "Debtors" Perhaps these days, banks are a little more circumspect about this but frequently I see the banks deciding that this is a good business and lend it money on the basis of the assets disclosed in the balance sheet without inquiring into the quality of the assets.

In reality what this executive is doing is simply digging a deep hole and as the old saying goes, when you are in a hole stop digging.

It is one thing to borrow on the basis of a balance sheet when there is a "cash flow" problem but before a decision is made to borrow, what should be done is to determine why there is a cash flow problem because sometimes the cause of cash flow problems are terminal and borrowing only deepens the hole and the mess.

What I like to do when I go into a troubled company is to graph the closing balances of the bank statement(s) over a period of three years. Before I do that I check to see if there are any aberrational transactions that might affect the balance, such as increased borrowings or capital injection, and then remove them from the study. When I present this graph to the owners it looks like a slippery slide or the graph of the temperature of a day and night in the desert. It is in fact a slippery slope and unlike the temperature in the desert, the indications are that it is not going to improve tomorrow. I point out to management that in the absence of any reliable strategy to turn that graph around, there is absolutely no point in borrowing money because if there is currently no strategy to reduce the debt, borrowing more money will only aggravate the situation.

Invariably, businesses in this situation have followed the tried and true method for failure. When you talk to the staff, they recount their frustrations almost to the point of anger because they can see that if the management had taken a different course, or kept good people and listened to them, or responded to their enormous energy; that energy would have been spent positively in pursuit of the objectives of the company rather than expended in frustration, anger and resentment. However, there is an upside to that in that once it has been possible to identify with the problems and frustrations confronting the staff, it is possible to identify what needs to be done to turn the graph around. Because management is between a rock and a hard place, they have to agree to surrender control so that the change of direction that emerges from the study of the organization and the interviews with staff can be implemented with a sense of urgency. If the business was not so far gone, management would never agree to seek advice, let alone respond to it positively.

Once staff sees the changes that they have suggested being implemented, the enthusiasm and energy suddenly become directed to the objectives of the organization and it isn't long before the graph turns up. But that is another story.

AVOIDING THE TRAPS

Profit and Loss and Balance sheets are history books written by the people in the organization. Once the figures are there, unless they have been fraudulently prepared (often called "cooking the books", as in Enron) they can't be rewritten in much the same way as you can't rewrite history. People can interpret history in different ways and from different perspectives and we can interpret financial statements in different ways and from different perspectives, but you can't change history and go back in time. So what is important is to operate the business so that the profit and loss account and balance sheet not only represents a true picture of the financial state of the organization but also a healthy picture. What we need to learn is how to construct an honest and healthy profit and loss account and balance sheet

We have learnt that profit does not necessarily represent cash. However, a business cannot go on indefinitely without achieving a positive cash flow and a cash surplus otherwise it will not survive. It is no coincidence that one of the world's leading text books on financial analysis[2] devotes the first pages to this issue of cash. The author states:

> *"Profits do not equal cash flow. Cash – and the timely conversion of cash into inventories, accounts receivables and back into cash – is the lifeblood of the company. If this cash flow is severed or significantly interrupted, insolvency can occur."*

So how do we get a decent profit and loss account and balance sheet?

Let us look at what is called the cash business cycle. Suppose you start off a business with $1,000 and you use

---

2   RC Higgins, *Analysis for Financial Management,* 9th edn, McGraw Hill, 2009.

that money to buy inventory[3]. You then don't have cash but in the balance sheet it would show that you have stock worth $1,000. You then decide to sell the stock at a 50% margin and you are a bit like the sports wholesaler in that you give customers thirty days to pay. Suppose it takes thirty days to sell your stock and then another thirty days to collect the money. The sale brings a paper profit of $500 but it takes thirty days to generate those sales and it takes another thirty days to collect the money. Accordingly, your $1,000 is out for sixty days, during which time you have to run the company. Suppose it costs $5 a day to run the company. This means that while your initial investment of $1,000 is out for sixty days without any money coming in, the cost of running the business is continuing at $5 per day. In the sixty days that the $1,000 is owing, costs add up to $300. That means that your CASH profit for the sixty days is $200 ($500 gross profit less the $300 cost of running the company). There are roughly six periods of sixty days in a year with the result that if you repeated this performance throughout the year, you would make an annual profit of $1,200 but this would not all be cash because there would be only five cash periods in the first twelve months.

The profit and loss account is going to look something like this:

---

3   For simplicity sake, we are going to make some heroic assumptions here because on close analysis the figures I am going to use are not quite accurate. For instance I am allowing for expenditure of $5 per day for the cost of running the business but I don't indicate where that money is coming from. In the end, it comes out of profits but it is unclear from the example where it comes from at the start.

P&L

Sales	9000
Cost of sales	6000
Gross profit	3000
Costs	1800
Profit	**1200**

And the balance sheet will look like this:

Balance sheet

Assets	**$**
Debtors	1500
Liabilities	
Bank debt	300
Net assets	**1200**

While the profit and the net assets are the same, the fact is that at the end of the year you owe the bank $300 and the reason is that the last sixty day's sales are represented in debtors and not in cash, but in the meantime you have had to pay the ongoing costs of operations to keep the doors open. So, you started the year with positive cash and at the end of twelve months you owe money to the bank. Let us hope that the customers pay their bills on time, otherwise you will be in a precarious situation.

In the meantime, a guy who is a well-known sportsman and understands business comes along as a competitor with similar product, but this competitor understands the necessity for cash and so he adopts a different business model. To him cash is king and he would prefer to make a smaller profit so long as he was not outstanding cash. So, his business model is to sell the same inventory at a 20% mark-up but no credit. He says, "You are getting a fantastic deal in that I am cutting my margins to the bone, but in return, you have to pay cash. This is really fair to you and it is fair to me. If I operate according to this business model, everyone wins".

So he starts with an inventory of $1,000 with costs of $5 a day and surprisingly, he turns his stock over every ten days. People simply can't believe his prices. While he doesn't expect to make as much money as his competitor, who has a 50% margin, he still hopes to do well and at least meet his main goal of having cash rather than debtors.

At the end of the year his accountant presents him with his figures and the profit and loss account looks something like this:

	P&L
Sales	42000
Cost of sales	35000
Gross profit	7000
Costs	1800
Profit	**5200**

And his balance sheet will look like this:

Balance sheet

Assets	**$**
Debtors	
Cash	5200
Liabilities	
Bank debt	
Net assets	**5200**

He is staggered. He is not only making more money than his competitor at a lower margin but he doesn't have any debt. The reason is that he is turning his stock over every ten days, which is thirty six times a year, less the last ten days in respect of which he will not receive his cash until the following year.

There are several lessons to be learnt from this. The first is that turnover is more important than margins. The quicker the turnover the quicker you get your money and the quicker you get your money, the better your cash flow.

The second is that by extending credit, you are exposed to higher risk than if you don't. Indeed, in the situation that this aggressive business man found himself, it may be that the people who paid the higher margin to the competitor did so because they didn't have the cash and were attracted to the credit. The third is that by developing a business model with the intention of always having a positive cash flow, a certain freedom of action is available to the business. It is not always behind the eight ball financially and it is amazing how businesses like this seem to create a staff enthusiasm which is self-perpetuating. While the staff in most cases are amply rewarded they seem to get a buzz out of being part of the success. Not only that, the sound financial position enables the business to embark on new initiatives which become another source of excitement.

THE THEORY OF
THE ORGANIZATION

Between November 1931 and May 1932, a most extraordinary investigation into the workplace was conducted at the Hawthorne Factory of Western Electric in Chicago. The factory produced telephone and associated equipment for the Bell Corporation. In those days all of the individual parts were manufactured and assembled on the spot. The factory employed thousands of workers.

The investigation was conducted in association with Harvard School of Industrial Psychology, headed by an Australian, Elton Mayo. Specifically, it was one of his senior people, Fritz Jules Roethlisberger, who managed the programme, and together with a co-worker, William J Dixon, published their findings in the monumental and seminal work *Management and the Worker*[1]. This work was not published until 1939, some seven years after completion of what have become known as "The Hawthorne Experiments". The delay in publishing arose out of objections by Western Electric which had in fact commissioned the investigations.

---

1 Roethlisberger & Dixon, *Management and the Worker*, HUP, 1939.

Some nineteen years before the Harvard Investigators commenced their Hawthorne project, another seminal book on management by an industrial engineer, Frederick Winslow Taylor had been published called *The Principles of Scientific Management*[2]. We will talk more about these works shortly but now, I merely want to introduce the historical context in which management approached the concept of the organization[3].

Subsequent to the industrial revolution and the massive expansion of manufacturing in the United States at the turn of the last century, the organization of the workplace and particularly the manufacturing workplace, was considered to be a mechanistic institution. By this I mean an institution that engaged people to undertake repetitive tasks that were assumed not to require thought but which demanded a commitment to these repetitive tasks. In return, workers were paid a salary not infrequently related to their productivity[4] In this context, Taylor came up with an explanation as to how to make workers more efficient and in a loose sense, the technique of time and motion studies emerged whereby the individual steps taken by people performing different tasks were measured so that the most perfect mechanistic process could be adopted, thus creating efficiencies. In this sense, the "Human side of enterprise"[5] as Professor McGregor ultimately described it, was inconsequential.

Taylorism became the buzz word and continued in

---

2   F W Taylor, *The Principles of Scientific Management,* Elibron Classics, 1911.

3   It is interesting that Drucker's work *The Concept of the Corporation* received similar treatment from the management of General Motors which Drucker used as the basis for much of his book.

4   The system was called the "piece work system".

5   See p. 72.

popularity throughout the twentieth century and beyond. It has its current iterations in the techniques such as Quality Control, Six Sigma and Quality Assurance, although these have modified to a certain extent the outrageously insulting perceptions that Taylor had of the worker.

Accordingly, in the late twenties, the Western Electric Factory approached the Harvard School of Industrial Psychology to examine their Chicago operation in order to determine the extent to which mechanistic changes in the workplace might bring about improved productivity. Worker fatigue was one area of interest to them; not so much that they cared about the workers getting tired, but they were concerned that mechanistic measures might limit productivity. Regrettably, this is where the Hawthorne experiments became synonymous with lighting and the association has continued to this day. In fact, the experiments had nothing to do with lighting although, in one experiment, there is a reference in an interview with a worker who explained that the reason for his slow work was to do with poor lighting in one corner of the room. It turned out to be an excuse for deliberately reducing his output. In fact, Western Electric had apparently conducted some experiments themselves with lighting, with no indicative results and decided that it would be better for the experts at Harvard to undertake the project.

The experiment of 1931 was one of eleven experiments and consisted of a group of men assembling transformers in what was called The bank wiring room. In brief (and the documentation of the experiment covers about one hundred and seventy pages) what the project revealed was that workers, who stood to benefit by increasing their productivity and who had the capacity to seriously increase their productivity, decided not to do so. They had an awareness of what was expected of them by management and achieved an output that met these expectations. On occasions, when they mistakenly increased output beyond the measurement that they believed was expected, they would make adjustments to lessen the output to bring it in line with expectations. Thus their reasons for controlling output had to do with a distrust of management. They believed that if they increased output, one of two things would happen. Either management would sack some of their work mates or alternatively, increase what was known in those days as the "bogey". The "bogey" was a benchmark of productivity against which their remuneration was measured. If the "bogey" was increased it would mean that the men would have to work harder for the same amount of money.

Without the knowledge of management, these workers informally organised themselves to achieve an output that they reckoned secured them against the sack or having to work harder for the same or less money. It became identified in managerial terms as "an informal organization". There was absolutely no equilibrium between management and the worker with the result that the workers, upon whom management depended to achieve financial performance, actually withheld their services without management being aware. Management was completely unaware of the fact that the factory was capable of greater productivity and accepted the output as in line with predictions and expectations.

This sad result was brought about because management in those days, and regrettably to a great extent today, do not understand what we can call "the theory of the organization". This is despite the fact that significant contributions to the learning in this area were made in the thirties. Studies in this area of what we might call the "mechanistic function" commenced before and continued after the first World War but most of these works have disappeared from the bookshelves of management schools, or if they are still on the shelves, they are not read.[6]

Of particular concern in the investigations at Hawthorne were the physical aspects of work, such as fatigue, which has attracted a great deal of research before, during and after WWI in England even to the point of measuring heart rates etc. However, what all this research established was a correlation between shorter hours of work (for instance reducing the twelve and a half hour day to ten) and the reduced incidence of industrial accidents. These mechanistic measurements were in the minds of Western Electric Management when they called in Harvard. Indeed, Elton Mayo, *who was head of the School of Industrial Psychology at Harvard*, in his book *The Human Side of Industrial Organizations*[7] dealt extensively with this area of investigation under the belief that in addressing the physiological needs of the worker, he was addressing the Human side of enterprise.

A little earlier in the Hawthorne programme, at Western Electric, the researchers had undertaken another and more extensive investigation into the work place. This particular experiment involved taking five woman out of one large segment of the factory that produced relays. Each woman

6   For instance, in writing this book I was a visiting Fellow at a major international management school with an extensive library. There were no books in the library on the Hawthorne Experiments and certainly not *Management and the Worker*.

7   See E Mayo, *The Human Side of Industrial Organizations,* HUP.

in the factory sat at a bench and was supplied with the individual parts to be put together by them to make up the relay. Their remuneration was determined by the number of relays they could produce. The five women taken from the factory to participate in this experiment were at the upper end of productivity before being introduced to the experiment.

They were brought together in a small room (the relay assembly room) where they were largely unsupervised other than by the researcher who sat in the room with them. Up until then, they worked straight shifts from 7.30 am to 1.00 pm and then from 1.45 pm to 5.30 pm. They also worked from 7.30 am to 12 midday on Saturdays. Initially, they continued to work the same shift and then the researcher indicated that he would like them to have a break in the morning and again in the afternoon. They were not keen on this because they felt that it would reduce their productivity and hence their income. After some discussion and reassurance, the women agreed to a five-minute break in the morning and again in the afternoon. The workers rather than the researcher fixed the time of the breaks. They were incredibly surprised to see that their productivity increased rather than decreased. Throughout the twenty-eight months of the experiment, different measures were discussed with the women and implemented. On each occasion, productivity increased after implementing the new measures, with one exception. Late in the experiment, they reluctantly agreed to return to the work times that operated at the commencement of the experiment without breaks. While no increase in productivity was recorded, it was surprising that productivity remained where it had been before that particular change and significantly higher than the level at the beginning. At the end of twenty-eight months, the amount of relays assembled by the women increased significantly, while the amount of time they spent assembling, reduced substantially.

In the bank wiring room experiment, effort was made to ensure that the workers continued to work in the same environment as previously with the traditional management and supervisory roles so that little would change. It seemed that the observer was able to get the confidence of these men so that they became comfortable that they could share their secrets with him and to explain their reluctance to increase productivity.

In the relay assembly room, the women worked with the observer and discussed the programme as they went along, participating in the decision making process. At the same time, they were not subject to the constraints that operated in the factory and they were given to frequent exchanges of conversation, which led to external social familiarity and friendships. One of the women, in response to a question as to why they were so productive, replied, "because we have no boss bawling us out".

The experiments were lengthy and the data were detailed. There were eleven experiments in all. However, for the first time in this ongoing industrial revolution and what we now might call the post industrial revolution, the researchers started to make observations that explained the organization of business differently.

"Where social conditions of work are such as to make it difficult for the employee to identify his task with socially meaningful function, he

is liable to excessive response and diminished capacity for work...

It became clear that what the experimenters had been observing in the different test rooms and in the interviewing programme was essentially neither logical nor irrational. It was essentially social behaviour...

The results from the different inquiries provided considerable material for the study of financial incentive. None of the results, however, gave the slightest substantiation to the theory that the worker is primarily motivated by economic interest. The evidence indicated that the efficacy of a wage incentive is so dependent on its relation to other factors that it is impossible to separate it out as a thing in itself having an independent effect."[8]

The researchers were on to something, but as indicated, the book didn't get published until just before the outbreak of WWII and then nations were mobilised. Organizational theory was so irrelevant to the war effort that this branch of research was never again visited with the depth of Hawthorne. One beautiful concept that arose from the relay assembly room experiment was that even in a factory where people repetitively undertook the same tasks hour after hour and day after day, there was still the flickering of the human spirit and the yearning of people for the ability to express themselves in a societal way as distinct from being a worker in an organization expected to produce X

8   Dixon & Roethlisberger, *Management and the Worker,* HUP, 1939, p. 575.

quantities of something for $Y.

Despite the fact that the Hawthorne research was virtu-ally consigned to the dust heap of academic literature (find copies of it in your library!) an amazing thing happened during the war. Men went off to fight and for the first time in the industrial revolution women entered the work force in their millions occupying factory floors that hitherto had been occupied by men. These women, doing boring repeti-tive work, achieved levels of output that were quite amazing to the point that some commentators made the insulting observations that women were more suited to repetitive chores than men. If they had read *Management and the Worker* with some interest they would have been aware that back in the early thirties, Roethlisberger had observed that output is more likely to increase when the worker can identify his or her work with some socially meaningful benefit.

Shortly after the war this issue was picked up briefly by Peter Drucker[9] as an aside to his involvement with General Motors, but was not explored in any depth. Drucker referred to the mobilisation of women in the workplace during World War II.

Can you just imagine the passion of these women, many of whom had husbands, fathers, sons, brothers or boyfriends off fighting for their freedom and the security of the free world? The depth of patriotism was unbounded. The social benefit of work was to protect the boys at war and to save the nation. What greater social benefit, in the context of Roethlisberger's description could there be? "No greater

9   P Drucker, *The Concept of the Corporation,* John Day Company, 1946, pp. 156-157. There are more recent editions of this incredibly seminal work which should be compulsory reading for all executives.

gift ... than a man who lays down his life for his country". If ever there was evidence of the correlation between work having a social benefit and productivity, it is probably difficult to find. But there was an additional phenomenon going on in the factories during wartime and it was one of collegiality in a common cause. The women were linked in some informal social context that made them feel at one with one another sharing the same vision. I also have a suspicion that many of these women had previously worked in the home with a limited community experience and now, each day, they came together in a common cause in a vast community of other women. This social experience would otherwise have escaped them[10].

Drucker laments the fact that this patriotic fervour and social benefit had not continued in the workplace post war.

> *"In the relationship between worker, product
> and plant – the second area in which constructive
> work is possible – we should try again to attain
> in peacetime the same identification with the
> product and the interest in it that were the
> result of patriotic fervour and of the glamour
> of war production."[11]*

Drucker had a great ability to combine his literary style with incisive and penetrating observations to the point on

10 As I have indicated previously, I have interviewed thousands of people in the workplace over more than twenty years on a confidential, one-on-one, basis. Almost without exception, when I have asked people to tell me what they like about working in the business, they reply, no matter how egregious the management, that "they like the people". This persistent constant in the workplace supports the proposition that societal influences at work are critical to engaging the people in the objectives of the organization.

11 P Drucker, *The Concept of the Corporation*, John Day Company, 1946, p. 192.

occasions where he elevates the discussion to some beautiful level. For instance, in the context of this discussion it is worth quoting the following Drucker observation:

> *"The efficiency of an institution depends both on the efficiency with which it organises individuals for a community effort and on the extent to which it organises man for his moral victory over himself."[12]*

He adds more depth to this concept when he identifies the nature of the individual within the context of the Christian tradition that is so influential in American society. This defines the individual as unique and the unique individual seeks recognition for status and dignity. These observations seem to have been passed over for quite some time, if not permanently in some respects, in the development of the modern corporation to which reference will be shortly made. Drucker concludes:

> *"But the solution of the problem of function and status in the industrial system ... can only lie in giving him the responsibility and dignity of an adult."*

However, in 1954 a book was published which should have had far reaching effects in the development of the corporation, but sadly, while it has become recognised as a landmark in the history of psychology, its findings have had little impact upon the functioning of the organization.

The book was *Motivation and Personality* by Abraham Maslow in which he enunciated his theory of the hierarchy

---

12 P Drucker, *The Concept of the Corporation*, John Day Company, 1946, p. 36.

of needs of the human individual[13]. He came to the conclusion that people have certain needs which he categorised into what he called a "hierarchy". What was important in his works from the perspective of the organization (and he didn't have in mind issues of management but only issues of psychology) was the issue of motivation and the fact that human needs such as a need for food are the factors that motivate the individual.

For the sake of completeness, following is a summary of the hierarchy

Self-Actualization

Esteem Needs

Social Needs

Safety Needs

Physiological Needs

There is quite lot of debate about whether or not these needs fall into a hierarchy and some criticism of Maslow that his work was based on too small a sample but there are still many who believe that basically, irrespective of whether they fall into a hierarchy or a loose arrangement where one can precede the other or they can both be experienced at the same time, there seems to be little disagreement about the basic proposition that human needs are motivating. In

---

13 *Motivation and Personality,* Harper & Row, 1954. There are critics of Maslow, although they seem to be related to detail rather than his broad conclusions. It would appear that few disagree with the fundamental proposition that the human individual is motivated by needs and that included in those needs are physiological: (to satisfy hunger); security needs; needs to love an be loved and needs for community, as well as higher needs such as what he describes as self-actualization.

this context, it is interesting to see that one human need is the need for self-esteem. Nowhere in his hierarchy does he express a need for money. Money is a means of satisfying needs such as the ability to purchase food, clothing or an automobile. It is interesting to link the absence of this need for money from his hierarchy with the findings of the Hawthorne researchers that there was no substantiation of the proposition that workers were primarily motivated by financial incentives.

Let us now flick back to the Thirties of the last century. In 1938, a book with the title *The functions of the Executive* was published. It was written by Chester Barnard who had previously been CEO of AT&T. Barnard explored the concept of the modern organization in the context of the individual and stated the dilemma that confronted him in exploring the concept of the corporation thus:

> *"On the one hand, the discrete, particular, unique, singular individual person with a name, an address, a history, a reputation, has the attention. On the other hand, when the attention transfers to the organization as a whole, or to remote parts of it, or to the integration of the efforts accomplished by coordination, or to persons regarded in groups, then the individual loses his pre-eminence."*[14]

To the extent to which businesses operate or any institution for that matter, they do so through the organization, and the organization is nothing more or less than a societal community made up of the people described in the

14 Chester I Barnard, *The Functions of the Executive*, 30th edn, HUP, p. 8.

above quotation. However, from his own experience and drawing on the work of Roethlisberger (which was probably not published when Barnard wrote) Barnard detected an undesirable phenomenon in organizations as a result of this depersonalisation of the individual. His experience was coincident with the findings of Roethlisberger in the Hawthorne experiments in that underneath the formal structure of the organization which is the medium for management and control, there develops an informal organization that is much more effective in facilitating communications between the people in the organization than is the formal structure. We have seen this earlier when we talked about the bank wiring room experiments. However, according to Barnard:

> *"...more often than not those with ample experience (officials and executives of all sorts of formal organizations) will deny or neglect the existence of informal organizations within their 'own' formal organizations. Whether this is due to excessive concentration on the problems of formal organization, or to a reluctance to acknowledge the existence of what is difficult to define or describe, or what lacks in concreteness, it is unnecessary to consider. But it is undeniable that major executives and even entire executive organizations are often completely unaware of widespread influences, attitudes and agitations within their organization. This is true not only of business organizations but also of political organizations, governments, armies, churches and universities."*[15]

15 Chester I Barnard, *The Functions of the Executive*, 30th edn, HUP, p. 121.

I have often come across these informal organizations in businesses to which I have consulted. For instance, on one occasion I was consulting to a manufacturing company that was in great difficulties. Management spoke of the symmetry of the managerial structure with a production engineer, planning production; a logistics engineer planning logistics and a host of other functions, the totality of which resulted in messages and orders going to the factory, which was expected to do the bidding of management. From management's point of view, everything was in place to ensure efficient production and they didn't have any worries about that side of the business. Their concern was financial. Talking to the people in the factory a different story emerged. There were people in the factory who were industry legends in their field and knew what they should be doing, but were constantly subjected to the dictates of people in the "office" who didn't know what they were doing. As a result, they opted out and had other activities to bring them together as a community. One such activity was playing remote control car racing in the parking allotment before management arrived at work, rather than running production.

The modern organization exists because an aggregation of people can achieve that which is impossible for the individual operating alone. So, the organization is not an entity in its own right but an entity made up of individuals. To the extent that the executive attempts to organise these people into collective action in which they lose their individual personality, the organization suffers. Barnard accepts that the corporation has to offer the employee incentives, but just as was the case in the Hawthorne studies, the incentives

Barnard identifies as more motivating than others are not financial[16].

> *"The opportunities for distinction, prestige,*
> *personal power, and the attainment of dominating*
> *position are much more important than material*
> *rewards in the development of all sorts of*
> *organizations, including commercial organizations*
> *... Even in commercial organizations where*
> *it is least supposed to be true, money without*
> *distinction, prestige, position, is so utterly*
> *ineffective that it is rare that greater income can be*
> *made to serve even temporarily as an inducement*
> *if accompanied by suppression of prestige."*[17]

At this point in time, Maslow had not been heard of, but by 1946 all of these commentators – Roethlisberger, Barnard and Drucker, had identified the problem of the organization and it was anchored in a misunderstanding of the needs of the worker. There was this persistent theme that the worker responded only to financial incentives and all of these commentators demonstrated that this was false. They had anticipated Maslow.

Then, in 1960 another commentator entered the scene by the name of Professor Doug McGregor who at the time was Sloan Professor of Management at MIT. He wrote the book *The Human Side of Enterprise*. Basically, McGregor identified two theories of management which he called

---

16 This is not to overlook the necessity to adequately compensate people financially for their contribution. Indeed, people generally know when they are being shortchanged in salary, and to the extent that they are, it exaggerates their other concerns about lack of respect and dignity.

17 CI Barnard, *The Functions of the Executive*, 30th edn, HUP, p. 145.

Theory X and Theory Y.

A summary of Theory X is that generally speaking, people must be coerced, controlled, directed or threatened with punishment to get them to put forth adequate effort towards the achievement of organizational objectives. Perhaps things have mellowed a little since 1960, but in today's environment, Theory X might be restated in that management believes that it knows best how to develop objectives for the organization and knows how best to achieve them. Employees are the tools to achieve organizational objectives and to the extent that they work towards those objectives, they are rewarded financially. Indeed, there is widespread belief that the best way to induce people to achieve the objectives of the corporation is by financial incentives.

According to McGregor, the assumptions of Theory Y on the other hand states that:

1. The expenditure of physical and mental effort in work is as natural as play or rest. The average human being does not inherently dislike work. Depending upon controllable conditions, work may be a source of satisfaction (and will be voluntarily performed) or a source of punishment (and will be avoided if possible).

2. External control and the threat of punishment are not the only means for bringing about effort toward organizational objectives. Man will exercise self-direction and self-control in the service of objectives to which he is committed.

3. Commitment to objectives is a function of the rewards associated with their achievement. The

most significant of such rewards, e.g., the satisfaction of ego and self-actualisation needs can be direct products of effort directed toward organizational objectives.

4. The average human being learns, under proper conditions, not only to accept but to seek responsibility.

5. The capacity to exercise a relatively high degree of imagination, ingenuity, and creativity in the solution of organizational problems is widely, not narrowly, distributed in the population.

6. Under the conditions of modern industrial life, the intellectual potentialities of the average human being are only partially utilised.[18]

McGregor concluded from his wide experience in American industry that most organizations fell into the category of Theory X. In this he concludes that the productivity of the American workforce was very much less than its potential and that the only way management can harness that potential is by what he describes as selective adaptation to human nature rather than to make human nature conform to the wishes of management.

So, yet another commentator turns to the issue of incentives. In an absolutely penetrating analysis of financial incentives, McGregor points out that money paid to an employee can only be used outside the organization, whereas the employee wants to achieve satisfaction within the organization. That indicates that employees have other needs to be satisfied if they are to achieve their potential.

---

18 Prof D McGregor, *The Human Side of Enterprise,* 25th anniversary edn, Mc-Graw Hill, 1985, pp. 47–48.

Inevitably, McGregor comes to the same conclusion as the previous commentators we have mentioned, in that individuals who work in an organization are social beings and need to achieve those objectives to which the human person aspires in different degrees of intensity. Status, dignity, an opportunity to identify enthusiastically with the objectives of the organisation, rather than being a mere implementer of a part of strategy which has no wider social significance and the desperate desire to take pride in one's work and achievement. There is also the need for community, but that is often achieved, even in the least desirable managerial environment, by means of the informal organization.

From 1933 to 1960 there has been a recurrent theme that an organization is a societal being; that the organization of business is the societal tool for delivering social benefits to the community; that organizational objectives cannot be achieved without the effective input of the individuals in the organization and to the extent that people will contribute willingly and with entire commitment to the organization, their needs for recognition, participation in a worthwhile community, dignity, respect and enhancement of their self-esteem have to be met. To the extent that they aren't, the individuals suffer, as does the corporation.

What strikes me about all this is the consistency with which people from different disciplines at different periods within a space of fifty years came up with similar explanations of the organization of business. In one sense, apart from Taylor (who was preoccupied with the mechanistic theory), all of the others foreshadowed the findings of Maslow who envisaged environments that would provide all of the opportunities for people's self-fulfilment. He did not relate this to the workplace although he wrote a later book that did so[19]. While Maslow did make observations about developments in industry he was more concerned with the relative inadequacy of our society to provide the opportunities that he considered so essential for the wellbeing of the individual.

So, here we know what creates productivity and the question is "to what extent are we practising what we know in every day affairs, particularly in the affairs of the organization?"

We will look at that shortly.

---

19 See *Maslow on Management*, John Wiley & Sons, 1998.

A SHORT DETOUR IN PHYSICS

For the moment, I want to take a detour into physics. In physics, there is a concept called "the conservation of energy" which states that energy can neither be created nor destroyed. Sounds like perpetual motion, which it isn't. I don't know much about physics but a famous scientist by the name of Richard Feynman[1]gives an excellent description of the principle in the reference listed below.

Imagine an ejecting machine (something simple with a pullback spring which, when released connects with a projectile and ejects it forward) being used to eject a ball bearing. Let us suppose that the machine exerts exactly the same amount of energy, every time it operates. A ball bearing is placed in the machine and it is ejected across a smooth table. After a while it becomes stationary. What has happened is that before the spring in the ejection machine is released, it has, together with the ball bearing, what is called "potential energy". Once the spring is released, the potential energy is converted into what is called Kinetic energy until all of the potential energy is spent. We retrieve the ball bearing and

1   R Feynman, *Six Easy Pieces*, Penguin, 1998, Ch. 4.

once again place it in the ejection machine but this time, while the spring exerts the same amount of energy as the last time, it ejects the ball bearing across a rough surface and the ball bearing becomes stationary a lot earlier than in the previous ejection.

So, what has happened? Energy can neither be created nor destroyed. Where did the energy go in the second ejection? The answer is that part of it went in heat, which is another form of energy created by friction, which slowed the ball bearing down, and that friction created heat. In physical terms, if you could measure the heat and the energy spent by the ball and add them together, they would equal the potential energy before the ball bearing was ejected. However, in physics, there is almost always a loss of energy because of friction and the potential energy is never converted completely into the end result of whatever you are doing, be it driving a car and combusting fuel into energy or simply rolling a ball along a table.

Friction takes something away from the system with the result that potential minus friction equals the distance the ball bearing will roll after it is ejected.

I hope you are with me because organizations are systems that possess potential energy, management is the ejection button and the surface is the cultural environment. It is important to realise that this is only conceptually so and it is not suggested that the effective operation of an organization is influenced by laws of physics. The organization, as we have seen, is a human social entity. Nevertheless, the analogy does make a conceptual point. An organization has potential. Any outcome that an organization wants to achieve equals, but cannot exceed, its potential. Perhaps we can state it mathematically as follows:

$$O \leq P$$

However, we know that in all systems, there is friction which means that it is pretty close to impossible for anything or anyone to completely achieve their potential. Friction will always cause some energy to dissipate. Now, if an organization can't achieve more than its potential and we know that there is always friction, it means that organizations will always achieve less than their potential depending on the amount of friction. How on earth can an organization experience friction? Ask Roethlisberger or Barnard or Drucker or McGregor or Maslow!

Just as the day is about to begin in the organization and everyone is at their desk or office or station, it is like a huge ejecting machine waiting poised to eject these people across their daily paths. The potential energy is enormous, but is contained within the hearts and minds of the individuals employed in the organization. That is what is being released. But suppose, in our ball bearing analogy, as soon as the ball is ejected, someone puts their hand out and stops it. The friction is enormous in relation to the potential because it prevents the ball bearing going anywhere. All the energy ends up in heat in the hand that stops it.

Some organizations are fantastic, but there are many that aren't, even though they might be satisfying investors and their shares might be doing well on the exchange. But to the extent that management is preventing people in the organization realising their needs (and as we know, most needs are other than financial and relate to self-respect, dignity and fulfilment in pursuing a social good); friction, or a better word, frustration, comes into play and is like a hand stopping the ball bearing in its trajectory.

Now, I am going to say something quite outrageous. I have consulted to commercial organizations for twenty-five years and before that I practised as a lawyer. In the course of my work, I have interviewed thousands of people in the workplace and in every case, people have complained to a greater or lesser extent that they are frustrated and the reasons for their frustration is that management does not communicate with them and decisions are made and things happen that affect them but about which they are not consulted. Often it is worse than that, in that people feel the decisions are crazy and the work practices could be much better if management would only consult with them. In this environment, people feel that they have little or no control over their own destiny.

What is surprising about all this is that when I ask people what could be better or improved, they always talk about issues that could improve the business and make their own life more meaningful. Do they complain about their wages? Rarely and if they do, it comes way down the list. Generally speaking more people complain about their remuneration when their work circumstances are poor. The more demeaning their work circumstances, the more aggrieved they are at their remuneration because they feel that if they are to be treated as they are, they at least ought to be paid for the insult.

Money is rarely raised by people as a major complaint in organizations. The frustrations they experience in their work and their inability to do their work as they feel it should be done and could be done are the major irritants or frustrations. Where does that leave us? It leaves us with the formula as follows:

$$O = P - F$$

This means that any outcome or, if you like, KPI of an organization is equal to the potential minus the frustrations. If there are frustrations in an organization, the outcome is going to suffer. That is why people like Roethlisberger, Barnard, Drucker and McGregor bemoan the fact that the productivity of industry could be so much more than it is today.

When I go into an organization, I concentrate on the F because I know that if I can reduce that factor, the O looks after itself. We will look at some of the outcomes that have been achieved in this approach.

We know all this stuff and have empirical evidence to support it, and yet time and again we see companies that flatly refuse to take any notice of the material. In a later chapter we will talk about the Boeing Corporation and how it has blown $250 billion in revenue, partly as a result of treating staff as mechanisms. Hire them when you want them and sack them when you don't, but expect them to be available again when you want them. Boeing experienced five major strikes in twenty years costing billions of dollars in short-term revenue not to mention the loss of market share to Airbus as a result of being unable to satisfy their customers.

South West airlines is unionised but its employees have never gone on strike but in fact love the company for which they are said to have made sacrifices[2].Many of the employees hold equity in the Company.

If you could just get it through the thick heads of management of many organizations that $O = P - F$, the world would be a lot better place and companies would be doing a lot better than they are at present. That is not to mention the tremendous improvement in economic activity that would follow.

However, we are cursed with the mantra of shareholder value and many CEOs worry that even missing a quarter in hitting numbers can damage their compensation package. As a result, there is so much concentration on immediate outcomes rather than sustainable outcomes and this is often accompanied by lay-offs, cost cutting, going short on resources, ignoring warning signs and risk taking just to meet the expectations of Wall St. In the meantime, the entire theory of the organization as a societal being responsible for the wellbeing of those people who make it work is ignored with the result that the people upon whom management is dependent to make the organization work, give it short shift because management fails to understand their needs.

---

2   I have heard a story that in an earlier oil crisis, staff offered to contribute some of their wages to offset the increased costs to the company so that it could continue to make a profit.

A CASE STUDY: BOEING

Immediately post World War II and for a period of approximately twenty-five years thereafter, the large commercial airline market was virtually saturated with players. The history of commercial aviation since the war reads like an edge of the seat "who-done-it", with the added spice of reality in which many have taken breathtakingly expensive haircuts but mostly at the cost, either directly or indirectly, of the taxpayer. And there are some pretty big names amongst them.

The Vickers Corporation of Great Britain had a winner with what was called a "Turbo prop" plane that was dominant for some time on shorter routes and this was followed by a large international model called the "Britannia". Anyone heard of Vickers aircraft these days? Then there was the De Havilland Comet manufactured by the British aircraft company De Havilland. It manufactured twenty-one of the planes and seven crashed, killing all on board and that was the end of the Comet.

Then a combination of British and French ingenuity produced the Concorde, the worlds' first and only commercial supersonic aircraft. Seven were produced and after serious environmental problems and a fatal crash in Paris resulting in the death of all on board, none are any longer in service.

Lockheed was a famous name in aircraft production and a leader in the industry. It produced a turbo prop plane called the "Electra" which entered the industry full of fanfare because of its increase in speed on conventional aircraft and shorter travelling time. It kept crashing and killing passengers and crew. Ultimately, production ceased.

Then of course there was the giant of them all, McDonald Douglas. Starting with the DC3 the company had tremendous success. It followed that success with further popular planes such as the DC4 and the enormously successful DC9, its first commercial jet.

Anyone heard of Boeing? It had been in business in Seattle since 1916 making a series of planes, some of them commercial and many for them military. It manufactured the famous B29, a long-range bomber plane in WW2. However, no one paid much attention to Boeing in the commercial field until 1963 when it introduced its first commercial jet with the name 727. This was followed by the 707 and then in 1970 the famous 747 entered the market. In ten years, Boeing had turned the large commercial aircraft market on its heels. Lockheed and Douglas tried to stay in the race, both producing large twin aisle aircraft but the 747 was industry disruptive and Lockheed exited the field, while Douglas ultimately merged with Boeing.

Boeing's brilliance had knocked out its serious competitors and the world was looking rosy. Dominance is a tricky role to play and there is a tendency on occasions for people in dominant positions to become "arrogant" which is a dangerous state of mind because it tends to place people in a state of denial.

Having achieved a startling realignment of the industry, Boeing didn't think much of an announcement in the early nineteen sixties on behalf of a French, English, German and Spanish consortium that it was going to enter the large commercial airline industry. Some at Boeing didn't take this at all seriously, given the poor history of the Europeans in the commercial airline market. The penny didn't drop even when the A 300 was introduced in 1972. This was Airbus's first commercial jet plane. It attacked a market segment not covered by Boeing or the ailing Douglas Corporation.

Since then, Airbus has taken 50% of the large commercial aircraft market and then some, which, over the past ten years, amounts to something like $250 billion[1]. What on earth happened to Boeing?

A great book has been written about the battle between Airbus and Boeing[2]. It is a well-researched book by a well-informed author and goes into great detail about the contest between Boeing and Airbus. However, the reason for introducing this saga into this discussion on management is to examine it in the context of competing concepts of costs as an impact upon profits, as against costs as an investment in sustainable growth.

---

1 The total of annual revenue announced by Airbus on their official website.

2 J Newhouse, *Boeing v Airbus,* Knopf, New York, 2007. There is another excellent book about the history of Boeing which discusses in detail issues surrounding the relationship between Boeing executives and its employees including the Unions: E Rodgers, *Flying High: The Story of Boeing and the Rise of the Jetliner Industry,* Atlantic Monthly Pr, 1996.

In an article by Lester Thurow[3] he compares the Anglo-Saxon/American corporate philosophy with that of the European (which he equates with the Japanese):

> *"In the Anglo-Saxon variant of capitalism,*
> *the individual is supposed to have a personal*
> *economic strategy for success, while the business*
> *firm is to have an economic strategy reflecting*
> *the wishers of its individual shareholders. Since*
> *shareholders want an income to maximise*
> *their lifetime consumption, their firm, customer*
> *and employee relations are merely a means of*
> *achieving higher profits for the shareholders.*
> *Using this formula, lower wages equal higher*
> *profits – and wages are to be beaten down where*
> *possible. When not needed, employees are to be*
> *laid off. For their part, workers in the Anglo-*
> *Saxon system are expected to change employers*
> *wherever opportunities exist to earn higher*
> *wages elsewhere."*

Whether or not this is an accurate summary of the Anglo/American corporate philosophy is not relevant to this discussion. What is relevant is whether the philosophy has application to the corporate approach by Boeing and to what extent this corporate approach has had some influence on surrendering such a huge market to a European competitor.

Since 1989 there have been five major strikes at Boeing ranging in duration from 42 to 69 days. In 2000, the

3   It is interesting that Drucker's work *The Concept of the Corporation* received similar treatment from the management of General Motors which Drucker used as the basis for much of his book.

engineers went on strike allegedly because of the contempt with which they were treated by Boeing management. When they threatened to strike, it was reported that management made the comment "Engineers never strike" which was in fact the case. Nevertheless, they did strike and caused enormous damage to production.

Boeing maintains that the unions representing most of their blue collar employees and the engineers are militant and just want to screw Boeing. However, the frequency of strikes and the anger of workers even to the point on occasions of rejecting Union recommendations not to strike, suggests that Boeing has to assume some responsibility. The strike in 2008, which caused serious delays in the manufacture of Boeing's newest plane, the 787 (which became years behind in production, resulting in serious cancellation of orders) was attributed by Boeing management as one of the causes for the Company losing money in that year.

It has to be said that the commercial aircraft manufacturing business is studded with booby traps, none the least of which is the volatility of orders from year to year. Below is a graph of the orders for Boeing and Airbus over the past twenty five years.

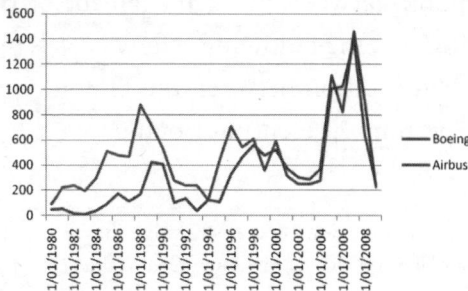

From year to year there is no consistency. Over 800 one year and less than 200 a couple of years later! How on earth do you plan for such volatility? Boeing, in the strictest sense of the Thurow criteria, would pink slip thousands of workers when orders were down, and then when the orders roared back, would hire them again providing they were still around. To many, including Wall St, it makes sense because of the preoccupation with quarterly figures. But does it make sense? If it results in blowing $250 billion in sales over ten years and permanently surrendering market share to a competitor, perhaps it doesn't make sense.

What is interesting about the above graph is that Airbus experienced the same volatility and yet, it never had a strike and its philosophy was to maintain its experienced work force[4]. As commented by the people at Airbus about Boeing:

> *"Airbus employees are critical of Boeing's habit*
> *of laying off thousands of workers in the slack*
> *periods and then rehiring those who haven't*
> *slipped away to work for a competitor."[5]*

In a report in Business Week in September 2005 during another standoff between the management of Boeing and the Union (IMA)[6], the following reference was made by the author to a conversation between the Union representative and an HR person representing Boeing.

---

4   In late 2009 there was a one day strike at Airbus in which workers protested the laying off of employees due to the down turn in the economy as a result of the financial crisis

5   J Newhouse, *Boeing v Airbus*, Knopf, New York, 2007, p. 10.

6   Industrial Machinists Union of America.

"Underlying the current standoff are the poor relations Boeing has long had with the IAM. That became clear in last-minute talks between Calhoun and Blondin just before the strike began. The two were deadlocked over yet another relatively minor issue, involving worker training. Blondin recalls asking: 'I just don't understand why you always fight us.' Blondin says Calhoun replied: 'You just don't get it. We represent Corporate America. You represent labor. We are always going to be adversaries.' Boeing says Blondin's account was taken out of context."[7]

Boeing certainly has had some HR issues in the past ten years and long before that. Managing staff of tens of thousands of people to ensure the effective manufacture and delivery of highly sophisticated aircraft and ensuring the adequate resourcing of the company must be quite a challenge. The following graph indicates how both Airbus and Boeing have handled that challenge. The graph is one of the employees of the companies as at the 31 December in each of the years indicated.

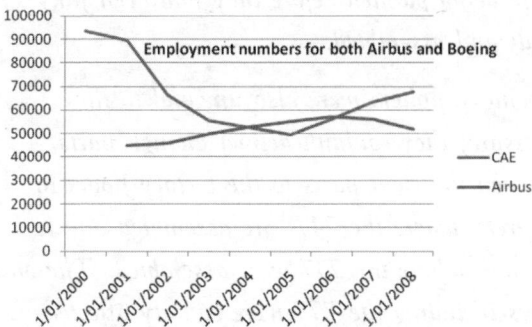

---

7   *Business Week*, September 2005.

We see Boeing shedding forty thousand jobs between the year 2000 and 2005, only to add twenty thousand between 2005 and 2008. What is interesting is that at a time when Airbus was taking over the lead in market share, Boeing was adding jobs and Airbus was shredding them. However, the graph clearly demonstrates some consistency on the part of the employment figures for Airbus but the opposite so far as Boeing is concerned.

Earlier, Boeing had already experienced difficulties. In the early nineties there were a number of economic issues that resulted in low order numbers, but in 1995 and 1996, orders came roaring back. The orders were beyond the capacity of Boeing's resources. Boeing hired thousands of people but production problems verged on the catastrophic. Newhouse comments

> *"Finally, in 1997 the industrial equivalent of a tsunami struck Boeing. The production line couldn't keep pace with what was called 'the steepest production increases since the dawn of the jet age' ... The factories seized under the strain. Airplanes got out of sequence. Some were being painted before they had been fully built and assembled.*
>
> *Boeing suppliers were also unequal to the pressure; they couldn't deliver enough parts, or even the right parts to the factory floors in Everett, where the 747s are assembled and in Renton where the 737 were assembled. The other lines including the 777 were equally affected ... Angry mechanics and machinists were calling the*

press, saying they were working triple shifts and
still behind. But the factory bosses, when called,
would say 'Everything is fine'."[8]

Understandably, the problems got into the market place and consistently the perception of arrogance on the part of Boeing management emerged. The dramatic layoffs had caught Boeing with their pants down and when it experienced this enormous increase in orders, it had to turn to staff that it previously sacked and ask for help.

In the meantime, Airbus started to benefit from the chaos at Boeing. It had seriously lagged Boeing in orders. For instance, in 1995 it received orders for 106 aircraft, whereas Boeing received orders for 441, but in 1996 Airbus received orders for 326 planes as against Boeing's 708; however, that was the largest number of orders received by Airbus since 1991. Boeing had let Airbus in the door and by 1999 Airbus outsold Boeing for the first time.

At Boeing there was growing antagonism to Airbus resulting in severe price cutting but this didn't affect Airbus which was able to meet prices and better them. There was a continuing belief at Boeing that things weren't fair and that Airbus was relying on government subsidies, which, to a certain extent, was true[9]. However, the argument missed the point that Airbus was doing something better than Boeing; it was able to manufacture planes more efficiently and less expensively than Boeing. Boeing did some benchmarking against Airbus. Newhouse attributes to Condit, the CEO of

8   J Newhouse, *Boeing v Airbus*, Knopf, New York, 2007, pp. 127-128.

9   Airbus maintained with equal and justifiable vigour that Boeing was also the recipient of massive government support through its defence research and development budget.

Boeing at the time, the following statement:

> *"One of the most dangerous places to be is number one. You tell yourself our technology is better, our costs are better and the other guy is cheating. You have to be brutally honest with yourself. We should have said what we know – that Airbus is doing a lot of things superbly. That was not a great light bulb going on and off in our heads."[10]*

A Boeing executive commented to Newhouse:

> *"It is not that way at Airbus. An Airbus guy can get an answer immediately and rarely has to bring in one of the top guns. Also, the Airbus people have more authority because they are higher level guys. Customers can raise a question and get an answer immediately. It's people have easy access to the top management. The Boeing process is very complicated."[11]*

In the end, the figures tell the story and it must have been obvious to Boeing that, to use the phrase of one Boeing executive "they had a cost crisis".

Following is a table of the ratio of staff to revenue of both Boeing and Airbus over the period 2000 to 2008.[12]

---

10 J Newhouse, *Boeing v Airbus*, Knopf, New York, 2007, p. 130.

11 ibid., p. 29.

12 I have been unable to obtain the revenue or staff of Airbus for the year 2000.

YEAR	BOEING	BOEING		AIRBUS	AIRBUS	
30/12/2008	68	28.2	0.41	52	38.7	0.74
30/12/2007	64	33.3	0.52	56	37.1	0.66
30/12/2006	56	28.4	0.51	57	33.2	0.58
30/12/2005	49	21.3	0.43	55	26.2	0.48
30/12/2004	53	19.9	0.38	53	27.2	0.51
30/12/2003	55	22.4	0.41	50	24.2	0.48
30/12/2002	66	28.3	0.43	46	20.3	0.44
30/12/2001	89	35.1	0.39	45	18.2	0.40
30/12/2000	94	31.1	0.33			

The numbers in this table are reduced to small numbers so that for instance, 68 in the first Boeing Column represents 68,000 employees and the 28.2 represents billions of dollars in revenue. The figure in the third column is the ratio of these numbers.

What this table demonstrates is that the ratio of revenue to staff was always higher during this period at Airbus than at Boeing and significantly so. By way of example, you will see in the forgoing Table that in the year ending 30/12/2008 the ratio of revenue to staff at Airbus was .74 and at Boeing it was only .41. The other interesting aspect of this Table is that the ratio at Airbus continued to improve at a faster rate than has been the case at Boeing. This tends to confirm the opinion of Boeing that Airbus was doing something "superbly good". Even though Boeing entered into a price war with the intention of knocking Airbus out of the race, Boeing was not successful and the above figures indicate why. It is amazing that when these figures are publicly available, Boeing seemed to ignore their presence or pretend that they did not exist.

This is but a brief introduction to the breathtaking story

of these two colossi in aircraft design and manufacture. There are many more parts to the story and quite a substantial segment of those stories is contained in the book by John Newhouse. However, the point of the material presented here is to examine this managerial preoccupation with cost as an impact on profit.

There is no doubt that Wall St loves companies that announce they are going to reduce costs by layoffs and to a certain extent it becomes a self-fulfilling prophecy. Announce layoffs and cost cuts and the stock prices respond positively and then the stock options of the executives are worth something. But one wonders if any of these smart people ever stop to think of the consequences of their conduct. It is one thing to produce good quarterly numbers (although Boeing has fallen by the way on occasions as has Airbus), but it is another thing to value the business in the context of its sustainability and longevity.

If it is the case (as it seems to be) that Boeing tend to look upon their employees as a cost rather than as an investment, and this has had some influence on their inability to satisfy customers, resulting in the loss of market share to a new entrant, it is necessary to ponder what might have been. It is all very well in a good year to record a profit of say $2.2 billion and another thing to ask the question of what might have been the case if the company had taken a different tack. Suppose it had worked with the Unions as did South West Airlines and integrated them into the company as though they were not only part of the company but a welcome part of that company. What if they had recognised in their employees the potential to generate sustainable and competitive growth rather than a nuisance who they didn't want around when things were down[13]? Perhaps they might not have experienced as many hiccups as they did and they may never have surrendered such a significant portion of the market to Airbus. Then, it may have been that instead of recording revenue of $28.2 billion in 2008, they may have recorded $38 billion as did Airbus and then Airbus might have recorded $28 billion.

When a company looks upon an item of expenditure as an impost on profit rather than an investment in the business and its people, including its customers, it will lose sight of the longer term consequences of the action because management will be constantly fixated on the short-term. In the longer term, management might proudly get up before the shareholders at the AGM and report a decent profit and dividend, but they will never overlay on that report what might have been, had they resourced the company better. Amazingly, everyone will go away happy with the quarter's figures or the final accounts and never ask "what would the accounts be like if we had taken a different tack in how we treated our employees?" Do you know, I think that no one ever asks that question! They certainly don't at Boeing, although I suspect that there are a few executives who privately ponder what might have been.

The die seems to be cast at Boeing. They have had enough strikes and appear to have run out of patience in dealing with Unions. It is all too hard. Their most recent plane, the 787 (which, by all accounts is going to be fantastic and a threat to Airbus) will be put together at Seattle

---

13 It is interesting that in an article in *Business Weekly* in relation to the most recent strike, the author of the article examines the position of the parties and concludes that the Unions request was a pittance in the overall scheme of things with the result that the author could not fathom what Boeing was all about.

for the time being although a huge portion of the plane has been outsourced to Japanese and Italian suppliers. The Japanese construct the wings, which in the past, were one of the great technological achievements of Boeing. More recently, Boeing announced that it will shift an assembly plant to North Carolina and engage non-union workers. I don't know whether it has occurred to Boeing that non-union workers have hearts and minds and families like union workers. However, what these moves demonstrate is the preoccupation of Boeing with the mechanistic side of enterprise which suggests that they have not learnt one lesson from the disaster.

The failure of Boeing to ensure a continuity of resources for the purpose of satisfying customer orders has had a serious impact on its financial performance and status in the large commercial aircraft industry. In 2009 it received 59 cancellation of its new flag ship the 787. One of the reasons for delay in completion (certainly not the only one) was the sixty-two day strike of machinists. Another reason for the delay may have been its decision to outsource much of the production with the result that logistical problems could weigh heavily on effective performance. But one suspects that the functions have been outsourced to teach the unions the lesson that Boeing can go elsewhere and is not dependent upon the workforce that has been its backbone for so many years. If that is the case, then it is a sad day for industrial relations. That is not to dismiss the claims by Boeing that the unions are a pain in the neck, but in a history of five catastrophic strikes in the space of twenty-nine years, one would have to wonder to what extent the interest of the customer was uppermost in the minds of the executives of Boeing.

MARKETING

I don't know if anyone has ever done a study of the ratio of books on marketing to the total books and literature published in relation to management, but in the absence of such knowledge I would guess that marketing would win by a few city blocks and the material ranges from snake oil to academic obfuscation and just about everything in between. Given the phenomenal failure rate of new products (I think the chances of success are roughly equal to the chance of winning on the poker machines) the value of this collection of wisdom is doubtful.

Having said that I believe that there are some successful gems to which reference will be made but anyone interested in seriously pursuing the subject as a discipline might need to go beyond marketing and spend a bit of time looking at the concept of economics. For the purpose of this chapter, I merely want to touch on some of the more fundamental issues relating to marketing that perhaps will point the way in our journey of understanding management.

I am not given to definitions, the reason being that once something is defined, exceptions are immediately discovered that corrupt the definition. In such a juvenile study as marketing (juvenile in the sense that it has only in recent times attracted the attention of academia, whereas we have had science as a serious discipline from the earliest times) I believe that we are a long way off from understanding it sufficiently to even attempt a definition. However, I think that it is not inaccurate to say that it is a process by which the enterprise of the organization is managed so as to deliver to customers, benefits, such that they will happily pay for them and in doing so enable the organization to profit. You might remember the definition of exchange earlier in this book[1].

In one sense it is not clear where the concept of marketing begins and ends in the operations of a business. For instance, it includes being in the right place at the right time; positioning the business so that it demonstrates a clear and favourable differentiation to others in the market; promotion which involves signalling the benefits to the market and pricing, which involves pricing the offering so that it is attractive against other competitive offerings.

Before we move on in this discussion of marketing it is necessary to introduce a concept identified by Michael Porter[2] which is known as "The Value chain". A simple description of the Value Chain is that of a chain which brings about the ultimate result for the customer. It is a chain that involves the participation of the supplier, the internal operations of the business and the interaction with the customer. In these various entities, there are innumerable links all of which are critical in determining the ultimate outcome for the customer. It is like a bicycle chain. If a

---

1   See p. 23.

2   M Porter, *Competitive Strategies*, Free Press, 2004.

link brakes, the bicycle won't work. If links are damaged or not well lubricated, the chain is less effective than it should be. The value that is ultimately delivered to the customer is determined by the effectiveness of this chain.

Let us talk about this chain of events that brings the resources of the earth to the hands of people who convert those resources be they raw materials or ideas into something of benefit to the end consumer as a closed system. There is a law which is demonstrated by exerting pressure on an inflated bicycle tube at one point and resulting in an increase in pressure at every other point of the tube. This is a physical demonstration of what is called Pascal's law of the transmissibility of pressure, which says "if the pressure at one point of a confined fluid is increased by a given amount the pressure increases by the same amount at all other points throughout the fluid."

You run a hotel and go to extraordinary lengths to plan the customer experience so that the customer will feel that the exchange has worked so well that he or she will not only come back but tell others about their experience. The receptionist at the front desk is there on her own when ten people are waiting. Some want to pay their bill and check-out and are in a hurry, while others want to check-in. She knows that she has to create a customer experience, but hell, the phone starts ringing and she is all on her own. The finance guys have decided that the front desk can cope with only one person and have factored that into the budget. The customers are getting more irate and some of them take it out on the woman on the front desk. The customer experience disappears out the window. Letters of complaint follow and the boss sacks the woman on the front desk[3].

Management hires another front desk receptionist who lasts a little longer, but with the same result[4]. Complaints from customers, sacking and fresh hiring! "It is damned difficult to get good people these days" is the response of management without it ever occurring to them that the consistent failure of a number of receptionists to deliver a good customer experience might illustrate a more fundamental problem and one that has been completely overlooked in developing this great business model of delivering a great customer experience.

News travels and the bookings never achieve those projected by the finance people. That one failure in the chain of events puts pressure on the entire organization and the marketing strategy of creating a great customer experience has gone out the window.

Businesses can have the best marketing strategy in the world and the greatest business model and it can all come unstuck at one silly little point of contact. Marketing embraces the entire operations of the organization because in the end it is how all those individual parts of the enterprise come together that determines the quality of the end result to the customer. So often we hear manufacturing blaming marketing, or marketing blaming finance or sales or everyone blaming everyone else when things aren't going as well as expected. A dysfunctional environment is the antithesis of successful marketing. One tiny weak link in the supply chain and everything can come unstuck.

---

3   Regrettably, this is not an infrequent event in the hospitality industry.

4   Another annoying organizational deficit in many hotels is inaccuracy in the billing.

An aspect of marketing that is consistently overlooked is that of organizational effectiveness. Indeed, I suspect that you will not see the term in most indexes of marketing literature, despite the recognition that one misstep such as the failure to adequately resource a reception desk at a hotel or to train a flight attendant as to how to deal with an unruly child in flight can damage the message of the organization.

Organizational effectiveness is critical to the success of any organization and should be integral to any marketing strategy. For instance, the speed with which Motorola went to market with its Iridium[5] telephone placed such demands upon the organization that cracks emerged and on the day of launch, there were manifold problems to do with the equipment, the quality of connections, the pricing of the calls and inaccessibility to the system. People were putting out fires from day one. Now, the whole concept was probably flawed in any event, but it was killed from day one simply because of this tendency not to include organizational effectiveness in the marketing mix.

Some would say that it is included in the "Positioning" concept, in that superior organizational effectiveness is a distinguishing characteristic. Regrettably, that is not always recognised at a practical level, nor is organizational effectiveness a learning discipline in the marketing curriculum.

Jan Carlzon, formerly CEO of Scandinavian Airlines in a book entitled *Moments of Truth*[6] identified that there are critical points of contact in the day to day functioning

---

5   See details of the Iridium story at pp. 108-109.

6 .   See a detailed reference to the Scandinavian Airlines turnaround story at p. 122.

of any organization and that managing those moments is an integral function of marketing. Broadly speaking two approaches to this issue have emerged and one in particular has the ascendency at the moment. It is a process called "quality assurance". Have you ever been to a supermarket? The person at the checkout counter will go through a ritual of saying something like "How are you" and then, without receiving a reply, will proceed to check you through so as to get on to the next customer as quickly as possible. This is quality assurance and a person is trained to give everyone this greeting. For quite some time I attempted to engage the clerk at the checkout counter by saying "How about you" without getting a reply.

During the writing of this book, I am looking after myself in a University apartment, and so I go down the street to a supermarket called Fry's. They have a checkout clerk and a young person putting your goods into a bag. I bring my own bag and ask the checkout clerk not to use their plastic bags but to use my canvas back pack. She agrees and I say, "Thank you so much, you are under so much pressure and you are doing such a great job, I hope your boss appreciates what you are doing!" That is where you get a reaction because it is probably the first time in ages, if ever, that anyone has told that person they are doing a great job. The lad who packs your bag does a great job and I turn to him and tell him how appreciative I am of what he has just done for me and his eyes light up. When I go back the next time, of all the people who go through that store, they recognise me; smile, say "hello" not in the QA manner in which they are trained, but as someone who is pleased to see you. The lad goes to no end of trouble to pack your bag and you do have a real encounter with people. I would like to bet that the only feedback that those people get from management is the amount of dollars that goes through their till on a shift.

What motivation do people have in any organization to engage as people in these critical encounters? We spent a deal of time considering the theory of the organization and hopefully, it emerged from those discussions that the opportunity for people to engage in meaningful societal activities that reflect well on their self-esteem and enable them to achieve their potential as individuals is a significant influence in organizational effectiveness and productivity. This also involves the necessity to constantly listen to people in the organization and get their feedback.

Unfortunately, most organizations today only recognise the necessity to manage moments of truth by training people according to some QA process. One of my great friends is also my doctor and he works in a very busy and successful practice. There are times that I need to call him during working hours. For years, the person answering the phone in the clinic would let her enthusiasm show through in the way she answered the phone. We would have a quick chat and then she would put me through to my friend. Recently the business was acquired by a public company and the next time I called, I was greeted with a frozen response, no engagement and told that my friend was busy and couldn't take the call. I subsequently learnt that the new manage-ment had "trained" the receptionist how to take calls and dispose of them quickly. The moment of truth had become a QA managed procedure and the role of the individual was eliminated. You might remember the brief reference to the work of Frederick Winslow Taylor in the *Principles of Scientific Management* in which he measured each step of a process of a worker to scientifically manage the worker rather than to leave to the worker the discretion as to how he would do his job.

We are in the age of Taylorism revisited and the people in marketing haven't woken up, although some companies have.

Let me mention just two stories that I recounted in the section on the theory of the organization. The first was the observation by Drucker of the enormous productivity gains achieved by women working in factories during the war. The second related to the enormous productivity gains by the women working in the Relay Assembly room in the Hawthorne experiments. Taylor could have measured the functions of the woman in the factory during the war for its entire duration, but would not have been able to improve on their effectiveness and productivity. The reason is that these women were driven by a sense of national importance. They were committed to the war effort and there was an enormous social significance attached to their work. They were proud of what they were doing and frequently, their efforts were recognised in news releases shown in the cinemas across the country and in women's journals and other media. They also had a sense of societal solidarity with their other female workers.

The girls in the Relay Assembly room were special as they had been taken out of a workforce of thousands and became individuals, relating to one another in what they believed at the time was an important experiment. They were involved, consulted, respected and unmanaged. In other words, they were trusted to do their best. Week in and week out they did exactly that.

In the next chapter we will briefly touch on the story of Scandinavian Airlines where people gave their all to achieve a turnaround. The national carrier was losing market share to foreign carriers. There was an issue of national pride.

While organizational effectiveness is reduced to quality assurance measures, all marketing strategies and concepts, no matter how brilliant, will never achieve the promise of their potential. They will be become captive of the unimaginative mechanistic constraints that prevent people from answering the phone as an individual, while insisting that they do it as a robot.

The organization is a societal creature made up of individuals, who all have societal ambitions that might be as simple as doing something as well as they can in the hopes that customers will express their appreciation of what they have done so that they feel worthwhile. It might be as simple as hoping the boss will recognise what they have done and give them a pat on the back and tell them what a good job they are doing. When these simple ambitions are smothered by Quality Assurance and mechanistic measures that prescribe how a job is to be done, the ambitions of the individual are unsatisfied, the potential of the organization is thwarted and in order to pursue their societal needs, the people in the organization form their own "informal organization" that often has aims at odds with the objectives of management.

To be as successful as possible, any marketing strategy has to recognise the latent goodwill and potential of the people who ache for recognition and the opportunity to do something with societal meaning. We will talk more of this issue in the section on leadership.

MARKETING II

There is in fact a current theory of marketing and it is contained in a story that has done the rounds. In fact, when I was at Colombia I was having dinner one night with Professor John Whitney, who was a great guy. He was a friend and student of Edwards Deming. At dinner I said "John I have four rules of management" and he replied "well that's funny, I only have two. Rule number one is that the customer is always right and rule number two is if you forget it, go back to rule number one". The current iteration of that formula, which in a crude sense is the theory of modern management, is "listen to the voice of the customer"[1]

I believe that theory has limited validity. I am not suggesting for one moment that you shouldn't listen to the voice of the customer, however, sometimes the customer might be silent as was the case with the introduction of the steam engine, the wireless radio, the supermarket, the motor car, the telephone, the cinema and particularly the talking cinema as well as TV, the computer, the mobile phone and the iPod, to mention a few things that have come

---

1   See C Anderson, *Free: The Future of a Radical Price*, Hyperion, 2009.

on the market without so much as a whimper from the customer saying "I want radio and telephone etc.". There is now a huge segment of commerce dedicated to the supply to the market "things" the market has neither asked for nor expected. However, once these things hit the market, customers immediately identify whether they meet a "need".

"I simply have to have the latest mobile GPS, wireless down load, email connectivity and web access as well as TV connect and in addition, I would like to talk on the phone occasionally irrespective of where I am".

The consumer never asked for these things nor expected them but now that they are here they are a necessity. Entrepreneurs have traditionally anticipated wants and needs; some successfully, others with horrendous failure.

Motorola is an American icon in the communications industry. One day, a senior Executive was holidaying with his wife in the Bahamas. His wife wanted to call her real estate agent on her cell phone but could not make a connection. Had the holiday been within the United States, this story may never have eventuated. It is reported [2] that the wife commented to her husband "wouldn't it be great if, no matter where you were, you could contact people anywhere in the world, no matter how remotely" or words to that effect. No sooner said that done. What a great idea. Satellite engineering was pretty much the go at the time.

Motorola commissioned market research on the possibilities of such an idea and the indications were that within the first year of launch, Motorola would have a customer base of 600,000, which would be break even. The research indicated that the company would recover its costs in the first year of operation[3]. The calculations were on the basis of a call charge of $3 per minute. It was also estimated by this "market research" that by 2002 Motorola would have a customer subscriber base of 2.2 million. Motorola went ahead with the manufacture and launching of seventy two satellites. Thus was born the Iridium telephone.

In 1996 the Gallup organization conducted research and reported that the Iridium concept was seriously flawed. However, buoyed by market research, Motorola went ahead with the launch in 1998. The handsets cost $1,300 and the usage charged turned out to be $7 per minute. On launch, there were problems with the hand sets, they were terribly expensive and cumbersome and a few satellites failed.

In his book[4] Sir Edmund Hillary related how surprised he was one day when sitting in his lounge room in Auckland to receive a call from his son. "Where are you?" asked Sir Edmund. "I am on the Vinson Massif"[5] Hilary was dumfounded "How is it that you are calling me from there?" "I have an Iridium telephone". Now, there are not a lot of people who want to make calls from the highest Mountain in Antarctica, apart from that, despite the market research, there were not a lot of people who wanted to use the cumbersome, expensive Iridium, particularly when you could get an ordinary cell phone to make most calls at a fraction of the cost of Iridium.

Motorola had launched a public company to fund the operation and it went into bankruptcy in 2001 after suc-

3   R Nelson, *From Concept to Reality*, September 1998, Applied Technology Institute, <www.aticourses.com/sampler/Iridium_FromConcept_ToReality.pdf>

4   A Johnston, *Sir Edmund Hillary: An Extraordinary Life,* Penguin, 2007.

5   The highest Mountain in Antarctica.

ceeding in persuading only 55,000 subscribers to connect to their system. That is one of the most, if not the most, spectacular flops in corporate history.

The cell phone was already in wide use when Motorola decided to go ahead with its Iridium and in a real sense it was bringing nothing new to the market. What it was doing was leveraging off that segment of phone users who were constantly on the move so that they could be contactable and they could contact people, no matter where they were in the world. That market is much smaller than the market for general telephone usage. The fact that the project was plagued with difficulties both before and after the launch didn't help, nor was the financial deal very attractive given that you could make landline calls from most places in the world for less than the minute charge of Iridium. It is unclear how the market research reached its conclusions, but when you think about it, the Iridium was only going to be of use for people in very remote parts and that market segment must be quite small.

In the end, Motorola didn't lose all that much over the deal as they floated the company and the poor old sucker in the streets took the hit.

However, there are some serious lessons to be learnt from this. The first is that with any new idea the cost has to be balanced against the risk. The figures might look great on market research but there is always another scenario which we call "the worst case scenario". Market research is pie in the sky stuff. Ask someone if they will buy a mobile phone which they can take to and use from anywhere in the world and they might say "sure, great idea". The real test is will they buy it? They might say they will but when the day comes and they actually see the offering and have to put their hand in their pocket to fork out some money, they might just say "well, right now I really don't need a mobile phone that I can use anywhere in the world, so perhaps I will wait". This has to be factored into any product launch and you then have to ask "what is the worst case scenario?" The worst case scenario is that you won't sell a single item and at that stage the question is "how much will I lose if I don't sell anything?" If it is not a lot, and there is some hope in the market research figures, then it is not going to hurt much if the worst case scenario eventuates. But if you are spending upwards of $6 billion of other people's money, then it is time to pause and say "could we tolerate a worst case scenario?" That is when you need deep pockets and you shouldn't be looking to pass the risk off to external investors.

The next lesson we can learn from this story is it to get the thing right before launch. There are horrific stories of people rushing to get a product on the market as quickly as possible so that revenue will flow. There is a tragic story about a huge Ferris wheel built in the City of Melbourne Australia which cost $100 million. The entrepreneurs had successfully launched a similar Ferris wheel in the city of London. Construction was well over time and it is rumoured that the owners insisted that the Ferris wheel be in operation by Christmas to get the Christmas trade. Weeks after the launch the wheel had to be closed down because of a fault. It finally had to be completely dismantled and rebuilt. In the end, the launch date has been delayed by years at goodness only knows what cost.

The Total Quality Management movement has fallen on hard times. However, a lot of wisdom came out of that movement that is still incredibly relevant today. A Japanese authority, Kaoru Ishikawa wrote a book called *Total Quality Management the Japanese way*[6]. In it he discussed this issue of getting it right first time.

In fact, the Panama Canal is not a bad story in demonstrating the necessity for rigour and detail, not only in developing a marketing plan but in its execution. The Panama Canal was a great idea but Duplesses who had built the Suez Canal didn't understand the power of the mosquito. The malaria infection of the poor workers on the first attempt at the Panama Canal was devastating. Just a simple thing like a mosquito and all your plans are useless, not to mention the expense and human toll. It also turned out that Duplesses was a crook and had his fingers in the till.

So anticipating needs is not much fun if you get it wrong. The problem is that it is not possible to accurately anticipate needs for something that the market doesn't know exists. Accordingly, great care has to be exercised before too much money is spent on futuristic adventures in marketing.

There is a rule of thumb in marketing that enables risk assessment. It goes something like this:

1. The easiest sale is of existing products to existing customers;
2. It is more difficult to sell existing products to new customers;
3. It is even more difficult to sell new products to existing customers;
4. The most difficult sale is of new products to new customers.

---

6   K Ishikawa, *What is total quality control? The Japanese Way*, Prentice Hall, 1985.

Big scale launches are fraught with risks because of the publicity accompanying the launch. It is great if everything comes off but not so good if things don't turn out quite as you would expect. (Coca Cola had a disastrous launch of their new Coke).

For smaller organizations with less ambition it is wise to avoid wide publicity in the first launch and to seek out a small market where the new product can be tested. If it works, then you can take the launch to a wider market but if it doesn't work then not much harm is done. In the end, the only effective validation of market research is actually going to the market to see if it behaves in the way that the researches expected.

The products that are least likely to be successful are those when the promoter says "I have a great idea for you" without in fact testing if other people think that the idea is all that good. This is where risk management is important both from the point of view of minimising financial risk and unfavourable exposure in the event that something doesn't go quite right.

Before leaving the issue of marketing it is relevant to mention the concept of competition because marketing is about competing. In his seminal book on Competitive Strategies[7], Professor Michael Porter of Harvard identified that there are three and only three competitive strategies which are:

1. Niche markets;
2. Cost leadership;
3. Differentiation.

---

7   M Porter, *Competitive Strategies*, Free Press, 2004.

Few businesses have niche markets and if they do, they tend not to have them for long. Accordingly, to compete it is necessary to focus on the other two strategies which often are complementary. We will deal with cost leadership in Chapter 13.

Differentiation simply means doing something better than your competitor so that the offering to the customer has greater appeal than the offering of the competitor. That is why so much emphasis is given in this book to organizational effectiveness and to the necessity to constantly improve the benefits while reducing price.

THE HISTORY
OF MARKETING

The origins of marketing are probably shrouded in the uncertain history of the cave men where barter was the likely mechanism for exchange, but its emergence today as perhaps the dominant area of study in management schools and the increasing pre-occupation of major segments of commercial organizations is perhaps more a response to the phenomenon of modern competition. Marketing is demonstrated more by reference to corporate adventures and misadventures that are often captured in what academia call "case studies" and out of these studies a principle as ancient as the early *home sapiens* emerges.

It was so sad that a week before he died, Adam Smith ordered that all of his manuscripts not ready for publication be burned, resulting in the destruction of sixteen volumes of his work. One wonders what magic we may have found in that literature because it was Adam Smith who lent some science to the concept of the "market" and it has been upon his work that so much of modern marketing theory has evolved. And so we are left with clues and those clues do suggest that the origins of modern marketing were alive and well, albeit egregiously so, in the evolving western human enterprise.

There is the story[1] that on the 21 August 1621 twelve women, one a widow and eleven maidens, were sent from London to Virginia to be sold to bachelors pioneering the colony of the New World. The price was one hundred and twenty pounds of tobacco. While not an uplifting story, it nevertheless has all the marks of entrepreneurship on what in those days must have been a grand scale. The entrepreneur who embarked on this venture must have identified the needs of lonely bachelors in the New World and of the shortcomings of the English class society that would have condemned these women in England to a life of service (goodness only knows what awaited them in the New World[2]). Whether happily or not, the benefit to these women was release from a life of drudgery to the opportunities of the New World. The benefit of the bachelors was the feminine comfort in a hard environment and of course, the benefit to the trader was a valuable commodity called "tobacco". These typify the function of marketing.

However, history is ambivalent about the extent to which corporations learnt the simple lesson. Let us assume that these young women who were "shipped" to the New World were willing participants and that everyone lived happily ever after. It would be a story of what we call today "win, win" in that everyone got something out of the transaction. Whoever planned it identified the necessity for there to be

---

1   See R L Francis, *This Day in Business History*, McGraw Hill, 2005 p. 247.

2   See for instance, a description of the plight of frontier women in 'America in the 1830s' by de Tocqueville. A de Tocqueville, *Democracy in America,* University of Chicago Press, 2000.

something in it for everyone. That person identified the market segment and the need that existed in that segment and identified, not only the benefit that those lonely bachelors were seeking but also the source of the benefit and the value to be placed upon it. A brilliant marketing strategy! Regrettably, there have been less admirable episodes in the history of marketing that involved the exchange of humans for valuable consideration.

Another episode that demonstrates this fundamental and enduring principle that forms the basis of successful marketing occurred on the 5 July 1841. Mr Thomas Cook was heavily involved with the temperance league, which was having a meeting that day in Loughborough. Midlands railway had just completed a line to that town from Leicester. Normally, about fifty passengers would take the train. Cook approached Midland Railways and offered to get them five hundred passengers if Midlands would reduce the price to 14 pence[3]. Midlands didn't believe Cook could deliver, but in fact 570 teetotallers took the trip. The reduced price made a journey possible that otherwise would have been impossible; they were also able to attend a convention that was so important to them and the railway company made a lot more from the 14 pence than they would have made from the fifty or so people who would normally have paid 50 pence. This story contains all of the ingredients of modern marketing. It is interesting in that it anticipates the discovery of the cash business cycle and is a great demonstration of how lowering margins and increas-

---

3   There are conflicting stories about the price. Some sources say that the price was a shilling which was in fact twelve pence.

ing sales generate more profit[4].

A need will go unsatisfied unless there is a benefit that can meet that need. Needs are satisfied by corresponding benefits. I might have a need to buy a motor car, but I don't have the cash. The bank has the cash and offers to lend me the money. The money itself is not relevant to my needs; it is what I can do with that money. That loan from the bank benefits me by making it possible to buy the car. Once I exchange the money for the car, the car benefits me in that I can use it as transport whereas before I bought the car there were places I needed to visit that were inaccessible to me. However neither the transaction of the loan nor the purchase of the car would have taken place if the price of the money was too high or the repayment terms too onerous or if the car was too expensive. Price is an incredibly important component of the marketing mix and that is too often forgotten. How did Thomas Cook arrange for impecunious people to travel on a train without the railway losing money? He saw that volume would make up for the reduced fare. In those days, there was no competition, but despite that, the offer of volume persuaded a monopoly to do a deal and lower the price.

Thomas Cook went on to form what was to become a global enterprise providing solutions and comfort to travellers around the world. Initially, Cook identified the members of the temperance league as a market segment who had travel needs that were not being addressed. In addressing these needs by organizing tours both within England and gradually to Europe and the United States Cook became extraordinarily successful. He accidentally stumbled across

---

4   See discussion of the cash business cycle in Chapter 5.

a business model that marketers would die for. He found a huge segment that was not being provided for, being tee-totallers who had a great desire for confraternity within their means. Whether the population of that market segment would offer marketers the same possibilities today is another question. People were able to travel abroad who otherwise would never have contemplated the possibility and within a budget that they could manage.

What is interesting about all this from a marketing point of view is that Cook identified a need as well as a solution and that solution was within the financial means of a large proportion of the market segment. Google made the same discovery albeit as a result of serious and rigorous scientific investigations by PhD students, Larry Page and Serge Brin at Stanford in the mid-nineties. The web was and to a certain extent still is a massive collection of independent pages all seeking attention. These guys saw a market segment that was a little bigger than the temperance movement and which could roughly be described as the world's population. Such has been their success in fifteen years that the word Google (a misspelling from the word googol) has now entered dictionaries throughout the world as a verb.

One of the reasons for success has been the price. How much do you pay Google to use its search engine? Well, you pay for your ISP server etc., but no one pays Google anything to search the web. Google is *free*[5] and as a result dismantles the class society. There are organizations that crave recognition and are prepared to pay Google an incredibly low fee for that recognition which is related to what are called "hits". Because the potential market segment consists

---

5   See C Anderson, *Free: The Future of a Radical Price*, Hyperion, 2009.

of hundreds of millions (perhaps billions), you don't have to corner a huge percentage of the market or charge much per "hit" to make a killing. These guys have done what Thomas Cook did back in the nineteenth century. They identified a market segment big enough that would pay a small price approaching zero, for the benefits Google could confer upon them. What a business plan! Get a few cents from millions ever day. In 2009 Google's revenue totalled $24 billion and it was just a series of mathematical investigations fifteen years ago. To say that Google has changed the world is not an understatement.

Now, it is not every business that chases what might be called "the bottom" in so far as price is concerned. Indeed, there are some very successful businesses that maintain a margin over their competitors. For instance, Microsoft charges for its suite of Office software, whereas Google and Sun Microsystems make a similar product available free. Perdue chickens sell something as commoditised as chickens and yet charge a premium as against their competitors.

Talking about marketing is a bit like doing a big complicated jig-saw puzzle. In the puzzle, you have to examine all the individual parts in order to gradually build some cohesive framework. If there is a theory to jig-saw puzzles, it is quite elusive. We can get a glimpse of what marketing is all about by studying cases of what others have done in the hopes of constructing some cohesive framework out of the parts. We can learn a lot from the millions of stories that abound in relation to the success and failure of businesses, but for the purpose of this exercise, I believe that if we can just concentrate on the brief stories of Thomas Cook and Google, we will get a guide to what marketing is all about and then we can look at some of the parts to see how they fit in.

We talked about the organization as being a societal being[6]in that it is made up of individuals and operates in a community of individuals. Marketing has to be seen in the context of the organization because it is primarily concerned with the relationship that the organization has with society or at least that segment of society in which it operates. Since the days of Adam Smith, it has been customary to talk about this society in which organizations operate as the "market". The participation of organizations within the market is a bit like the biblical story "many are called but few are chosen"[7]. Many have come to the market with their wares since time immemorial but few have succeeded and it is important, in discussing marketing, to identify whether there is some element common to successful organizations.

However, before we go further I want to make a distinction between sustainable and unsustainable organizations. The corporate world is awash with fly by nights. Enron was a company that had found the commercial philosopher's stone. Bernard Madhoff was a Wall St wonder and had multi-millionaires and perhaps billionaires eating out of his hand. He was the Einstein of investment and consistently returned yields on investments way above the market until he ran out of other people's money and ended up doing three life times in prison (I am not sure how the Americans manage three life times). But by comparing businesses like Enron and Madhoff and thousands of others that came to the market intent on making money for the business with-

6   See Chapter 6.

7   Mathew 22.14.

out conferring adequate benefits on the people who paid them the money, we can put together some crude theory of the jig-saw of marketing.

Cook, Page and Brin saw needs in the community. The community that they identified as having these needs is what is called in marketing "a market segment". In the case of Google, that market segment was the world's population. Initially, in the case of Thomas Cook, the market segment was the temperance league. Identifying a market segment where a need exists that you can satisfy is the first step in marketing. Once a need is experienced by members of a community it becomes a social need and to the extent that it is a social need it can only be met in terms that satisfy or motivate the individuals in that society. We have learnt from Maslow the various needs for which the individual seeks satisfaction and unless an organization addresses those needs at a price that make sense to the needy, it either shouldn't go into business or if it is in business, it will eventually fold.

On 25 August 2003, *Business Week*[8] published an article after conducting a poll on the reasons for business failure and came up with six main reasons. Apart perhaps from the "inexperienced management" reason, all of the others are symptoms and not reasons. All businesses that fail do so because they run out of money. It is a bit like saying that all people die because their heart stops. There isn't any science in that. The question is why do they run out of money? The answer is that their expenditure exceeds their income. That is also a dumb answer; everyone knows that, so we once again ask "why does the expenditure exceed the income?" Almost invariably it is because the market (that society of people like the society of people identified by Cook, Page and Brin) felt that the benefit offered at the price didn't really address their needs. Full stop!

In any field of endeavour and learning there are exceptions. Try learning the Russian language and you will find that the moment there is a rule, it doesn't apply. That is why definitions are so useless because the moment you define something, someone will come up with an exception and they will be right. So, I am not saying here that there is a complete and definitive unexceptional principle that determines whether or not a business will succeed or fail. There have been cases where people have had a good product but have put their hand in the till and the business has gone belly up[9], but I believe that it can be said that an organization will be unsustainable if it continually fails to bring benefits to segments of society that have a need, at a price which enough members of that society are prepared to happily pay in order for the organization to make a profit. That is perhaps a lawyer's way of trying to cover all bases. You can put it another way. Sustainable profits can only be achieved by an organization if it continually brings benefits to its market segment that satisfy a need at a price that individuals (customers) are happy to pay. Even in cases where financial catastrophe causes bankruptcy, it is often discovered that the organization was giving customers haircuts and the customers resented the fact that attempts were being made to pull the wool over their eyes.

One of the reasons that monopolies are considered so

---

9   See the history of WorldCom for instance. It set the pace in telecommunications in the later part of the last century and the early part of this century until it went bankrupt over accounting scandals

pernicious is that even if they are acting in the best interest of the customer and not trying to rip them off, a perception lingers in the minds of the customer that a monopoly will never have the interests of the customer completely at heart. An awareness of this suspicion coupled with a persistent demonstration by monopolies that they didn't have the interests of the customer at heart has brought about the world of competition we are experiencing today.

Well, there we have the Coutts attempt to explain what marketing is all about. The organization of business is the instrument of bringing to the market, benefits that meet societal needs at a price which the customer is more than happy to pay and that also ensures an ongoing sustainable profit to the organization. Isn't it interesting that eighty years ago, Roethlisberger[10] identified that a principal need of the worker was to feel that what they were doing had a social benefit. Drucker followed that up in his *The Concept of the Corporation* when he referred to the productivity of women in the factories during WWII. Workers need to feel that they are involved in delivering a social benefit and customers have social needs that they want satisfied by the organization of business. Isn't that a neat fit?

In this context, marketing is the driver of the organization and should influence its direction and culture (about which we will have more to say).

In 1981 Jan Carlzon was appointed President of SAS (Scandinavian Airlines). He was a young man (forty-one at the time) who was in a hurry. SAS had fallen on hard times and he was called in to turn the airline around. There

---

10 Dixon & Roethlisberger, *Management and the Worker*, HUP, 1939, p. 575 and the discussion in Chapter 6: *The Theory of the Organization*.

were many problems with the airline and one related to its persistent inability to take off on time thus resulting persistently late arrivals at the destination. Strangely enough, business people in particular, who pay over the odds (and certainly did in those days) for service, one of which was to get to a destination on time, were unimpressed by SAS and were deserting in droves. Even the local Swedes were giving their loyalty to carriers with a different national flag. Carlzon discovered that there was quite a procedure to go through before a pilot could leave the departure bay and one of them was that he or she would not receive clearance until all the luggage was loaded on the plane. Because quite a few people were changing planes at Stockholm and because the SAS plane on which they had just arrived was late, it delayed the transfer of luggage from the arrival plane to the departure plane, thus ensuring the departures would be late. The whole thing compounded as customers were defecting and SAS was chalking up losses.

Carlzon issued directives that Pilots were to take off on time irrespective of whether luggage had been transferred from another aircraft. The Pilot would make the decision to leave the departure gate on time. This caused a bit of a problem for a couple of days as the Pilots exercised their new found freedom but as planes started to take off on time, they amazingly commenced arriving on time and because they were arriving on time they were taking off on time. Carlzon wrote a book about his experience and called it *Moments of Truth*[11]. He made the point that every contact a customer has with a person representing SAS was a moment of truth in which the manner in which the SAS person

11 J Carlzon, *Moments of Truth*, Harper Collins, 1989.

related to the customer had an influence on the perception of the customer to SAS. There is nothing particularly brilliant about that because it is just a straight out application of the theory of Michael Porter's value chain. The purpose of mentioning this is to bring attention to a fact that is frequently overlooked, which is that at any moment of truth, if it is not handled properly by the organization, what we call the value proposition of the organization is compromised.

The marketing strategy of Carlzon was to develop a level of customer service that would compete more than favourably with that of other airlines and this got down to simple issues of how the flight attendant or the check-in in clerk or the baggage handlers related to the customer. The marketing strategy required a cultural shift and this had to run right through the organization because every member of SAS carried on their shoulders the responsibility of living up to the value proposition. Organizational effectiveness is critical to the success of any marketing initiative because marketing initiatives are dependent upon implementation. SAS ran into trouble again because Calrzon had demanded much of the staff and they gave willingly. He rewarded them by sending them a wrist watch at Christmas time. I don't know how much the watches cost, perhaps a couple of hundred bucks. You work your but off for a guy and go the extra ten miles week in and week out and you get a wrist watch at Christmas time and this to airline employees who live on duty free. Ultimately, Carlzon had his moment of truth when the company went on strike.

Our friend, Clarence Saunders, who invented the supermarket and was dudded by Wall St had a comeback in the late thirties. He invented another supermarket in which the customer could select the item and have it placed on a conveyor belt which would take it to the check out and save the customer carrying all the stuff (they hadn't invented the trolley for super markets in those days). The idea was great and people flocked to it only to discover that the conveyor belt broke down and the whole thing didn't work. The business folded and I think that Clarence went bankrupt again. The idea was great and it had in mind the social benefit but its execution was terrible. That part of the marketing plan didn't work with the result that customers didn't see they were getting any benefits in addition to those enjoyed at the traditional supermarket.

Sustainability also involves recognition that times change and what might be a great social benefit today may not be tomorrow and it is about tomorrow that marketers are primarily concerned. By the sixties, Greyhound bus line was the dominant coach carrier in the United States. Gradually, it had to contend with a rapidly changing environment. Racial discrimination laws required it to alter its treatment of black people. Later, low-cost airlines entered the fray and Greyhound became involved in the traditional cost-cutting exercise of corporate America. As a consequence it suffered some terrible strikes, one of which went on for thirty eight months. It filed for bankruptcy and has emerged as a much smaller disciplined operation responding to the current environment. Greyhound made the same mistake that the Railway companies had made as the airplane started to attract customers. It believed it was in the bus industry, whereas it was in the business of transporting people to different destinations. Because it lost sight of the fact that the benefit being conferred upon customers was a cost effective manner of transporting people, it vacated a large segment of the transport market to low cost airline companies.

Then there are people with great benefits that are needed in the community but they forget to tell the community that they are in existence.

Marketing is a pretty tricky thing and it has a variety of faces. So, there are three principal aspects of marketing.

The first is being sensitive to social needs so that the organization can constantly measure its offering against market expectations.

The second is ensuring that organizationally, the business has the capacity to deliver on the promise and not mess up.

The third is to continually evaluate its internal capacity and resources to determine how they might be best utilised in innovation or bringing new products to the market in situations where no need for those products have been expressed by the market.

The sticker note pad developed by the 3M Company, the Sony Walkman and the Apple iPod are examples of the last aspect. These products emerged without any apparent predecessor and suddenly people thought "I need one of those". I call this the external function of marketing and will turn to it in the next chapter.

SCARCITY AND ABUNDANCE

Marketing is about economics, not strictly in the sense that economists would define the term, but in the common meaning of the term as in "is this economical or isn't it". This question is asked in relation to the market in which a business either operates or intends to operate. South West Airlines is studied perhaps more frequently than just about any other corporation. One reason is that it seemed to do the impossible for a new airline to operate in Texas, (which is the State where South West originally set up operations), because all studies indicated that the market was saturated, particularly by the long established Texas Air and the International Carrier, Continental.

However, these airlines charged full price in an industry where prices were protected. They also tended to fly from established airports with high fee structures. In addition, they sometimes serviced locals by allotting them seats on an incoming international flight which would be crowded and have the level of tidiness that international flights tend to have towards the end of the flight. This is not to mention the delays that were often experienced by their domestic customers.

South West identified that there were two gaps which, if they could fill them, would make it economical for them to operate an airline and economical for passengers to use an airline. The two gaps were the quality gap and the cost gap. Current airlines were providing poor quality at high cost, which indicated to the founders of South West that there must be a market for those currently using Texas and Continental within Texas and passengers who would like to fly but couldn't because of the cost gap between existing air and bus transport. Not only did South West take passengers from Texas and Continental, they also found an enormous new market in those who would like to fly but couldn't because of the cost. Their business model was to fly from low cost regional airports and to eliminate all the costs that were unnecessary on short flights such as food and beverages. The brevity of this story does not suffice for an adequate description of the South West operation but it is intended to be indicative of this issue of economics in marketing.

The law of supply and demand is frequently quoted as the basis for formulating pricing and it is, in my view, an unfortunately lingering concept in a world that has developed beyond the days of monopolies and quasi monopolies into one of technology and competition. What has emerged in its place is a more refined concept that might be called The Economics of abundance and scarcity. Technology and manufacturing practices have created the ability of businesses to produce abundance at significantly less cost than was the case twenty years ago. A two litre Mercedes Benz today costs tens of thousands of dollars less than a two litre model twenty years ago, but up until the financial disaster of 2008, Mercedes was more profitable than it had been in the past. The reason has to do not only with improved manufacturing techniques and technologies, but with the relationship between volume and price, which we will discuss in the *Management Accounting* sections.

The capacity to manufacture automobiles around the world has exploded, thus creating an abundance. This very abundance creates a scarcity in that there are not enough people for all the cars that are being manufactured, resulting in colossal bankruptcies.

At the extremes, marketing has to factor in the degree of abundance on the one hand as against the degree of scarcity on the other. Now economists, or at least some of them, try to tell us that markets work efficiently and markets will work out the right balance. That is like telling me that I can't lose money on the stock exchange and I can tell you a thing or two about that. In fact, if you could get published by writing a book about how you can lose money on the stock exchange I could write a best seller. Just by way of example have a look at this graph;

This is a graph of the Dow Jones index of thirty of the leading stocks on the NYSE over a five day period as I was writing this material. In the space of five days the index has oscillated between over 10,250 and 10,050. Can you imagine the billions of dollars in value that have been created and evaporated over that five day period? And economists tell us that markets are rational. Each second of the day, investors are relating the price of stocks, not so much to their intrinsic value but as against their best guess of the direction of the economy and the chances of particular stocks benefiting or suffering from that economic outlook. It is like putting money on horses at the race track. What were all these rational investors doing in a rational market when the Dow dropped 776 points in one day in 2008?

The law of supply and demand is a law that indicates with an increase in supply but with demand constant, the price should drop. In monopolistic situations, this rarely happens. There was a period in which the number of telephone subscribers increased without any decrease in the cost of a telephone call[1]. In some countries, the cost of electricity has gone up while the number of users has increased. In more practical terms, the law has been used to identify profit opportunities rather than growth opportunities. The law of supply and demand tended to be looked upon by some businesses as a technique for restricting supply in a market with growing demand. A great way of maintaining margins and profitability!

We talked about Google and its ability to develop abundance of supply in a market where there is an abundance of

---

1 It is surprising that in these days of mobile phones and calling cards, some hotels still charge exorbitant mark ups on the use of room phones for long distance calls. I wonder if the bean counters have done sums to see what the hotel would make on phone calls if the cost of using the phone for long distance was decreased and the number of users increased.

customers. Abundance chasing abundance is the antithesis of the perception that some businesses have of the law of supply and demand and it doesn't make sense if you want to make money. What was the revenue of Google in the calendar year 2009? There is no need to go back because I can remember. It was $24 billion. What we didn't mention in that chapter was the profit. It is all very well to chase abundance with abundance, but you have to make a profit. Google's profit for the year 2009 was $6.5 billion and this for a company that has been in existence for ten years. 25% net margin after all cost! That is more than a lot of organizations' gross margins and yet Google has abundance chasing abundance.

When South West came into existence, traditional market research indicated that there was no room to expand the domestic market in Texas. What they didn't realise was that the world has now moved into the stage of abundance chasing abundance and the trick is how to unlock the abundance that a business proposes to chase. This is not to throw out entirely the concept of the law of supply and demand but in its traditional concept the law or principle, tended to be anchored in culture that imagined limited supply against greater demand. That paradigm held good, only to a limited extent because businesses that controlled the supply or which were in industries where supply was limited and the demand was high had no incentive to become efficient and never profited to the extent that is now possible where abundance can chase abundance. In an economy where there is abundant supply and abundant demand, prices should be zero, but that is only true to the extent that there are sufficient competitors in the market who can produce a product at zero price and remain in business. The trick is to learn how to make a profit by being an abundant supplier for an abundant market.

Let us talk about scarcity for a moment and put to one side such brand names such as Bulgari and handmade Swiss watches such as Patek Phillipe because most businesses are not in the ether of exclusivity. A lot more believe that they can hide behind their brand image and leverage their margins however, I suspect that they have another think coming.

Different areas of the wine industry are experiencing this phenomenon. For instance, the geographic area of champagne in which wines with the name of "champagne" can legally be produced is restricted. Up until the financial tsunami, the champagne industry had achieved the limits of its production and decided that land which previously had been considered inadequate to satisfy the quality of champagne had miraculously become adequate thus expanding the geographic area of champagne. However, that was only kid's stuff to their internationalisation of their product. Much more sparkling wine is made by the champagne houses in the New World and countries like Chile, New Zealand and Australia than is made in France. Because there is an abundant market for sparkling wine, the Champagne industry is chasing that abundance by creating abundance of supply.

The world of marketing is now about realising the benefits of scale and has nothing to do with the limiting of supply to maintain margins. Strangely enough, this phenomenon had its commencement at the beginning of the industrial revolution which validated the promise of Adam

Smith that a collective organization of many people could, with the aid of technology (he never envisaged the explosion of the technological impact on production) achieve more than that of one individual operating alone.

Therein are the seeds of the organization, but it is well to remember that while the organization has its explanation in the application of people and technology for the purpose of mass production, the purpose of the organization was the pursuit of abundance and this abundance only exists where there is a societal need. Accordingly, even at the outset of the industrial revolution, business success was dependent upon meeting societal needs.

Once the new era was able to produce goods previously not in existence, there became an abundance of needs accompanied by scarcity of supply which resulted in many being excluded from the market while the entrepreneurs leveraged their margins to the hilt, never realising the opportunities by creating an abundance. Texas Air thought that it was impervious to competition and could gouge the market until South West understood that by creating abundance of supply and lowering the cost it could pull the rug out from under Texas Air's feet. Even with the emergence of the motor car, this belief in the ability of exclusivity and scarcity of supply to leverage margins persisted with the result that it was the belief of the abundant market that motor cars were the domain of the rich. Scarcity of supply became an established perception. That was until Henry Ford came along and exploded the myth of scarcity and since then more and more business organizations have come to understand that creating an abundance for an abundant market makes a lot more sense financially than creating scarcity in order to maintain margins. But the successful organizations understood the flip side of the deal and that was the necessity for accuracy in identifying the benefits that the abundant market expected, even if sub consciously, and providing those benefits at a price that would penetrate the abundant market. Moving from scarcity to abundance involved efficiency, which in turn involves organizational effectiveness. Organizations capable of leveraging their potential have been and will continue to be more successful than those who fall by the wayside in leveraging their resources.

With the ongoing intensification of the applications and cost of technology, the technological barriers to entry into markets are continuing to decrease and are reducing the technology gap between organizations. The SABRE airline booking system is available to many competing airlines and there are many cases where competing organizations use the same tools such as Dell or HP computers, Rolls Royce jet engines, Ericsson telephones, Customer Relations Management software, electricity providers, furniture manufacturers, suppliers of office software, utility providers, computer assisted drafting software, data bases for legal firms, manufacturing equipment and a host of other generic products that have multiple applications with different competitors. In theory, this technological equalising phenomenon should eliminate competition but it doesn't. It certainly creates the opportunity of extending the size of the market into abundance. However, some organizations develop sustainable business plans by constantly reducing price and increasing profits while others fall by the way side. It is worthwhile investigating why this happens. (One explanation lies in the fact that organizational effectiveness is a critical element of marketing)[2].

There is a traditional approach to pricing called price elasticity. This suggests that as the price of a product, commodity or service increases, the number of sales decrease to the point where the price becomes so high that no one will buy the product. I remember once being on a train between Brussels and Amsterdam. I hadn't eaten and was hungry. There was a guy on the train selling the most basic ham roll you could imagine and he wanted $7 for the roll when one would expect to pay about $1.50 in a shop, even in Paris. I could not bring myself to give this guy $7 and so he had a stale ham roll and I went hungry but had my $7. I wonder how much business he would have done and how much money he would have made if he had sold the rolls for $2.50?

There is a point where price becomes a deterrent to a purchase and the elasticity graph plots that point and all points in between so that people can maximise their sales and profit. Because theoretically, a high price means negative sales, the graph tends to be negative although it is said that some products are not subject to the law of supply and demand[3]. Theoretically, when the price is zero, sales are infinite like the repeated use of Google throughout the day and the week and the month and the year. When the price is infinite, no sales take place. Finding the happy spot in the middle that generates the most sales at the most profitable price is a fundamental driver of the bean counters in busi-

---

2   See Chapter 9.

3   Veblen goods, named after the economist Thorstein Veblen, tend to become more attractive as the price increases such as Rolls Royce motor cars.

ness. What they are missing is that the world has changed and it no longer works like that.

This tendency to think in terms of price and sales creates the risk of getting into the Bermuda Triangle mentioned in the section on *Management Accounting*[4]. When the demand closes in on the resources, there is stress that, if not addressed quickly, results in defection of customers and growth stalls if not retreats.

Let us look at a price elasticity graph.

Price elesticity graph

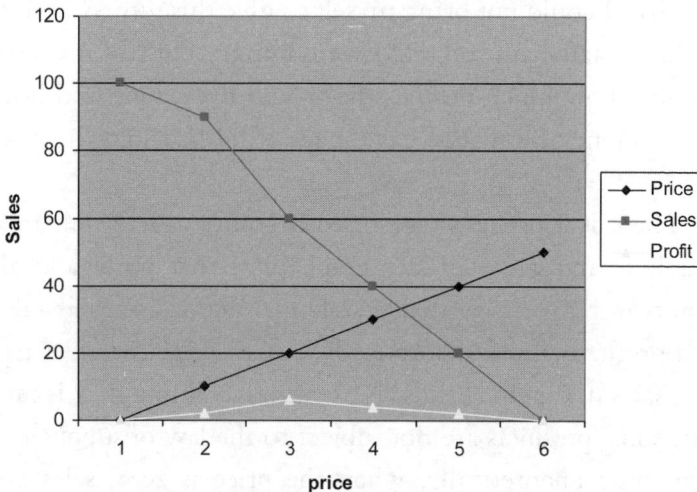

This is an unrealistic but representative graph which indicates that one hundred sales are achieved when the price is zero[5] and when the price reaches a unit of 50, sales are zero. Somewhere in between is the optimum number for

---

4   See Chapter 13.

5   This paradigm has now been flawed. See C Anderson, *Free: The Future of a Radical Price*, Hyperion, 2009.

sales and price and in the above graph it happens to be that the profit goes to 6 when the price is 20 and sales are 60. If management focus on this number they tend to become ecstatic when the business closes in on this number and the profits are maximised.[6] If we forget the price elasticity graph and concentrate more on what we might call a bang for a buck, we need to think about how much further we can go and this involves just finding out how big the market is. Now, following is a typical graph of the businesses that do not recognise where they are on the growth scale:

Abundance graph

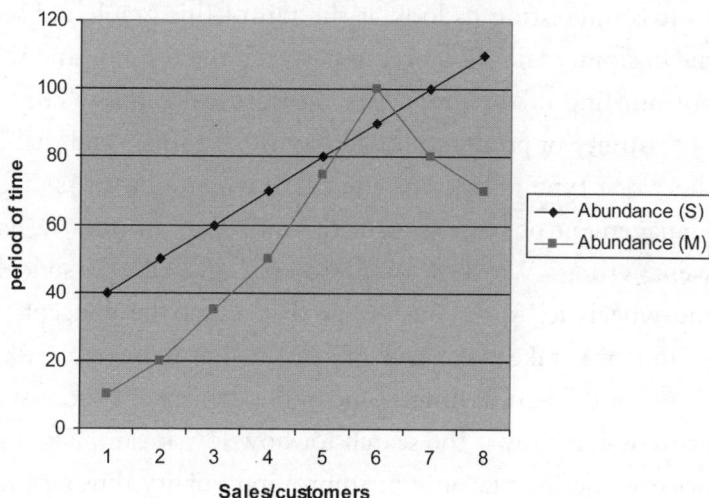

The line with the rectangular stops is a line of the production of goods or services and the line with the diamond stops is a line of the number of customers. What is surprising about this graph is that when productivity is at its high-

---

6   We will discuss this issue in more detail in the chapter on *Management Accounting I* p. 143.

est, customers start falling off. That seems to be contrary to my theory about abundance, but if you look closely at the graph you will find that it is very similar to the graph of the Bermuda Triangle in the section on *Management Accounting*[7]. In fact it is a Bermuda Triangle, because that is exactly what happens if a business is not adequately resourced. In order to create abundance, it is placing too much of a strain on existing resources in order to maximise profits. Even though the people in the organization achieve miracles, it is at the expense of customer satisfaction and the morale of the employee, with the result that the business never gets the benefit of abundance.

It is interesting to look at the tail of this graph and see the customer fall off. The gap between the top line and the bottom line of the graph is a measure of scarcity. This is not scarcity of product but scarcity of customers and that is the worst type of scarcity you can have in a business. The management of businesses in this situation ask me "What went wrong? We were doing so well and all of a sudden the wheels fell off". Businesses that adopt the concept of abundance, take risks and of course, businesses are risky things at the best of times. One of the drivers of a successful growth company is the search for how low it can make the price while maintaining or improving quality thus getting the business into speculation because it is in unchartered territory. The lower a business can go with price while maintaining or improving quality has the risk of getting market share while losing money. But let us think about this for a minute. Wal-Mart is a pretty successful business and it is said that sometimes their margins are only 2%.

7   See Chapter 13.

My goodness, how can you make a profit with such a low margin? As at December 2009 there were 810 Wal-Mart discount stores. Just take one product, say soup. Suppose each store averages sales of 500 cans of soup a day at $1 per can. The mark up would bring in .02cents X 500 that makes $10 by seven days equals $70 by 52 weeks equals $3640 by 810 equals $2,948,400 by how many thousand products? Just about everything Wal-Mart sells can be purchased at other stores but Wal-Mart sets the benchmark so far as price is concerned. Wal-Mart has discovered the skill of bringing abundant supplies to an abundant market. The greater demand, the lower the price. Say that again! Surely, the greater demand the higher the price because, after all, that is the law of supply and demand. This is the twenty first century and people who wake up to that will survive and prosper and people who don't...

It can be said that Wal-Mart and Google and similar industries might fall into this new paradigm but others don't. Take Bentley motor cars for instance. It is said that an exception to the price elasticity are certain luxury expensive "status" items[8]. The customers for this category of goods are said to include people who seek the prestige of owning something exclusive that not too many people can afford and so the higher the price, the more attractive the product. They might be right but there are probably millions of people who could afford to buy a Bentley and don't. One of the reasons is that having earned all that money, they respect it and take the view that the money for a Bentley motor car doesn't represent value to them. In other words, the benefit that Bentley motor cars can deliver to them is far

---

8   This category of goods is technically described as Veblen goods.

less than their perception of value for money. But Bentley is in fact in the price elasticity graph. We can produce so many cars for so much and make so much money. Suppose that they just looked at stepping costs and calculated how many cars they could sell if the price was $50,000 less per car. Now, certainly the market is not the world at large, but every product of merit has an abundant market, which is a market of all of the people who have the where-with-all to acquire the product. With a price discount without sacrificing quality, it may well be that Bentley could find ways of making the car for less and increasing sales well beyond their existing sales. In other words, they could go for abundance to an abundant market. But some customers might feel that they have been diminished. However, if a lot more customers are happy and Bentley is making more money it might just have to put up with the discontent of those who merely bought the car for status.

However, getting to the stage of penetrating an abundant market with abundance it is like trying to achieve the speed of light. It is said that theoretically, as an object approaches the speed of light it takes more and more effort to accelerate rather than less. In ordinary concepts of speed and acceleration, the faster the car is going, the less energy is required to make it go faster because it has momentum. However, it is said that as an object approaches the speed of light it requires infinitely more energy to accelerate, making it impossible to achieve the speed of light. Once you get down to a two cent margin or a few cents a click, you are approaching the commercial speed of light and it takes effort.

Given the equalisation of technology and the universal application of technology to competing businesses, what tricks are available to pursue this wonderland of abundance of supplies to an abundant market? There are roughly four resources available to any organization and they are:

1. Money
2. Technology
3. Commodities such as the resources of the earth like oil, copper etc;
4. People.

The first three resources are the same, no matter in whose hands they reside and it is their application that can make a difference. However, the application of the three first resources mentioned is in the hands of people and that brings me back to the section on "The theory of the organization" where we discovered that to the extent that we can reduce friction in an organization, more of its potential is released. On this theory, one has to believe that the less friction in an organization, the closer it will get to the management equivalent of the speed of light and increase dramatically the possibility of bringing abundance of supply to an abundant market.

Just imagine working in an organization that has as its mission the intent to constantly increase the benefits to its customers while reducing price. That is its mission and it shares that with all employees. However, more than that, it says to the employees, "you often know what can be done to do things better, quicker and cheaper and that is the difference we want to bring to the market so that we will be seen as a caring business, constantly seeking ways to improve the benefits we confer" and the company backs its promise with commitment so that employees feel that they don't have to put on some artificial uniform when they step inside the workplace and become something that management expects of them rather than who they are.

The potential of people in the work place is enormous but much of it is untapped. Reorganising the work place so as to release that energy is the challenge of management today because out there is an abundant market. That market will only be available to organizations that can achieve efficiencies that result in lowering costs as demand increases and achieving an ability to deliver abundance of benefits.

MANAGEMENT ACCOUNTING I

At the beginning of this book we looked at the nature of revenue and concluded that Revenue was proportional to the benefits conferred on the customer or at least those benefits that the customer perceived it receives in return for the price. We also talked about cost as an investment in creating benefits. We now want to look more closely at this issue of cost in the context of what is called Management Accounting.[1]

There is a tendency by many smaller organizations to look at costs in totality without relating those costs in discrete ways to creating value. The authors to whom I have referred in the footnote identify two types of activity that incur costs. One activity is a value–adding activity and the other is a non–value adding activity.

In its simplest form, a value adding activity is one that brings value to the customer while contributing to the profit of the business. A non–value adding activity brings

---

1 A lot of the material in this chapter is drawn from a fantastic book on Management Accounting (which happens to be its name). W Morse, J Davis and A Hartgraves, *Management Accounting*, Thomson, South Western, 2009.

no additional value to the customer and certainly does not contribute to the profit of the business.

That doesn't mean that you go through your accounts and have a witch hunt for non-value adding activities although it might be wise to look at some items of expenditure to determine whether they are business related or personal (such as the latest Mercedes Benz) because all of those costs end up being paid by the customer, either directly or indirectly. In many cases, non-value added expenditure will not jump out of the financial statements shouting "I am not value adding" because there will be some items of expenditure that are part value adding and part not. For instance, the salary of a receptionist who runs messages for the boss might also have the responsibility of taking phone orders. The time taken in running messages is not creating value for the customer whereas the taking of phone orders is, with the result that part of her salary is adding value and part not.

This chapter is not a lesson in Management Accounting but an introduction to the topic so that people are more aware of the issue of cost and the relationship of cost to profit. People who have a serious interest in the subject could do a lot worse than working through the text book of Morse, Davis and Hartgraves in addition to the text book of Professor Higgins mentioned in the Chapter 5[2].

In this discussion on cost, it is essential that people keep in mind the fact that there are positive and negative sides to the issue of cost. On the one hand, unnecessary cost reduces the opportunity for a business to reduce price and

---

2   RC Higgins, *Analysis for Financial Management*, 5th end, McGraw Hill. See also Chapter 5.

therefore unnecessary costs put a business at a competitive disadvantage. Unnecessary costs deprive the business of passing benefits on to the customer. On the other hand, costs can improve productivity or add in different ways to the offering of a business to a customer. For instance, the cost of providing a customer service help desk might be considered by some as unnecessary. However, if it is discovered that orders are falling off and further investigation reveal that people were defecting because they couldn't reach anyone in the company to help them with a problem, then it may be that had the business employed a customer service officer, they would have appeased the customer and detected a problem that could have been corrected before the defections occurred. In this situation the cost of a customer service officer could be seen as value adding.

Now that we are well into the twenty-first century, many people are realising that in many ways the commercial landscape has altered. This has had more than a little to do with the internet and the availability of knowledge about a range of competing products at different prices. Price has become a dominant issue in this fiercely competitive world with the result that cost management has to be undertaken in the context of competition. Too often, businesses that are confronted with ailing sales, for whatever reason, have two immediate reactions. One is to cut costs and the other is to increase "marketing". Neither of these in themselves are competitive strategies.

As we learnt in the segment on marketing, one view is that there are only three competitive strategies[3] which are:

3 See M Porter, *Competitive Strategies*, Free Press, 2004.

1. Niche markets;
2. Cost leadership;
3. Differentiation.

For the moment, let us talk about cost leadership. In brief, it means that a business that can produce a competing product for less than the cost of a competitor has a competitive advantage.

In 1982 the Swiss watch industry, which had dominated the clock industry since the middle of the 16th century[4], was facing catastrophe to the point where Swiss Banks, which less than most banks don't like losing money, moved in as unofficial administrators and pushed traditional management aside. What had happened was that Japan and America had learnt the relevance of quartz crystals in measuring time and recording it on the face of an analogue watch and with some precision, at a cost immensely less than the cost of producing a Swiss watch. The American Company TIMEX had their watches for sale in supermarkets at incredibly low prices. The quartz watch was industry disruptive.

The Swiss had ignored quartz technology and couldn't compete. Cost leadership had knocked them out of the water. The leading managers in the industry had another problem common to businesses that have been market leaders but get into difficulties. The leaders of the main watch companies had become complacent and arrogant. In the end, they didn't know what hit them[5]. Miraculously by virtue of the assistance of a physician, the Swatch emerged

---

4 Ironically, it was the insistence by Jean Calvin on austerity that resulted in the banning of jewellery in Switzerland and as a result the innovative Swiss artisans turned their craft to watch making in about 1541.

5 We will mention this issue again in the segment on leadership.

and the Swiss were able to make a comeback. But that is another story.

In an article in *Business Week*[6], the authors are quoted as making the following points:

1. Everything gets cheaper faster;
2. Cutting costs will be essential to successful competition;
3. Innovations build profit.

In this crude summary of the article there is a temptation to conclude that everyone has to go in with the hatchet and cut, cut, cut. For heaven's sake, never do that without using a little of the science to which reference will now be made and never do it without reminding yourself that costs need to be value adding and you don't cut costs that are in fact value adding. What we need to look at are what are called "Activity cost drivers".

An activity cost driver is a cost that affects the end result to the customer. For instance, in manufacturing, an activity cost driver could be the cost of raw material or a part from a sub-contractor. The Japanese resurgence in the automobile industry was partly due to extensive activity in integrating suppliers into the production process and eliminating logistic, communication and quality faults, thus giving the Japanese a lead both in relation to quality and price.

It may be of some assistance to describe the term "activity" in the context of Management Accounting. For the purpose of this discussion, let us think of an activity as the process that brings about the ultimate benefit for the cus-

---

6   See *Business Week,* 28 August 2000. (A summary of the article is contained on p, 12 of *Management Accounting* ibid).

tomer. In one sense the activity is represented in the goods and services sold to the customer. An activity cost driver is a cost involved in bringing about the delivery of those goods or services.

Any activity requires resources and resources are a cost. So, there are two types of costs.

1. One cost is a cost necessary to achieve a competitive advantage;
2. The second is one that is unnecessary and does not endow the business with a competitive advantage.

This distinction is very important because when businesses get into difficulties they tend not to make that distinction and throw the baby out with the bath water. I remember a company that sold industrial tools and one of its activities was to use a sales person to drive around in a van to factories and construction sites and sell tools on site. Accountants advised the business that this was an unnecessary cost and as a result, the business closed down that activity and sold the van. The bank balance improved temporarily, but then sales fell off dramatically to the point that lost sales were far greater than the cost of the travelling sales section of the business.

Different companies apply different criteria to cost. For instance major commercial airline carriers cater to a market segment that responds to full cabin service and a range of add ons such as frequent flyer points. They are more expensive than the discount airlines that cater for people who want the cheapest price. Extras are therefore important to a company seeking one market segment, but are unnecessary to airlines serving another market segment.

Having said that, it seems to becoming clearer as we get well into this century that lower cost airlines are more profitable, or, lose less money, than the traditional carriers. This phenomenon is not restricted to airlines and is being experienced in many industries as price competition has become ferocious. Accordingly, companies that have had long-term strategies of managing cost so as to ensure maximum benefits to customers have a distinct competitive advantage over companies that merely slash and burn when the economy tanks without altering their basic business model.

There are many businesses which sell multiple products and in order to carefully analyse the relevance of cost to products in such organizations, we move into complicated territory so, for the purpose of this segment let us assume that we are dealing with a company with one product line. If you go to the Morse, Davis, Hartgrave text book it will take you through in detail all you need to know about single unit and multi-unit sales.

In any situation there are four different cost behaviour patterns.

1. Variable costs. This represents an identical amount for each unit of activity. For instance, in the manufacture of a plastic folder, there will be a unit of cost per raw materials, which will be identical for each folder produced. Accordingly, the variable cost will increase with the number of folders produced. At the end of the run of folders, the total variable cost will be a multiplier of the number of folders produced and the unit price of the raw material per folder. It is amazing how often businesses don't

identity unit costs but just look at the financial statements such as the profit and loss account to get a synopsis of cost. The purpose of management accounting is to enable discrete measurement of costs and provide opportunities for savings or improvements that do not emerge from the financial statements.

2. Fixed costs. Fixed costs are more often than not unrelated to unit activity. For instance, capital equipment such as computers, software, printers or manufacturing plant, once they have been purchased go into the books as a fixed cost irrespective of whether or not they produce anything. What becomes important with fixed costs is the ratio of the cost to unit volume. The greater the unit volume the less is the fixed cost per unit and so the fixed cost varies according to the number of units. The greater the number of units, the less is the fixed cost per unit and vice versa.

3. Mixed costs. For instance, it is necessary to provide lighting for the general purposes of the business but the production of a unit might require power. The general power bill will be a fixed cost but the power per unit should be capable of measurement and it then becomes a variable cost. This area of cost and fixed costs give rise to quite a deal of argument in multi-site organizations where it is necessary to allocate say, head office costs, which are not in themselves income producing, across sites. I have generally taken the view, much to the annoyance of

the various site managers that the costs are allocated according to the gross revenue. While this means that the site which is generating the most income pays the most contribution towards the fixed costs of head office, it is much more equitable than requiring each site to contribute an equal percentage of the unproductive fixed costs.

4. Range costs. It is really important that people understand these costs because they can be strategically critical. If sales are within a certain range, say 200 to 400 it may be necessary to have X number of employees to service that level of activity. However, if the sales are at the lower end of the range, then the cost per unit will of course be higher than it is at the top of the range. If, the sales exceed that range, then it may be necessary to add employees so as to service that additional volume and at that stage, the costs move to another level. So, within the range, the costs are fixed but once the range is exceeded, the fixed costs go to another level.

Without wanting to be confusing, there is another cost with which we need to be acquainted called "marginal cost". The gurus have attached to this concept a tricky mathematical equation which employs the mathematical technique of calculus that is handy to measure the rate of change of things. I don't understand calculus and so I will try and convert this important concept into plain English.

Suppose you need X employees to produce Y products. However, if the business doesn't produce Y but a number less than Y, say Y-10 the cost of producing this reduced number of goods is obviously going to be greater than if X people produce the total of Y goods.

Let us give X the number 10 being a unit that represents the total cost of employing X people. And if Y represents 100 goods then the cost per unit (which we call the marginal cost) is obviously

$C = 10 \div 100$ which equals $1/10$ or 0.1. However, if X employees only produce 80 items, then the cost $C = 10 \div 80$ which equals 0.125.

This is all incredibly obvious but is so obvious that its significance is often overlooked. In any business there is a certain base resource that it needs in order to just sell one product but if it only sells one product, then it will be out of business pretty quickly if it doesn't have a load of money in the bank. Even if it has a load of money in the bank, if it can't sell enough units to reduce the marginal cost to less than the revenue, it will go out of business.

We now enter a really scary area of management and it is incredibly important to understand this concept of marginal cost and be able to apply it on an ongoing basis.

What we have established so far is that there is a unit of cost necessary in a business to support a range of activity, be it the manufacture of plastic folders or the delivery of legal or medical services. A range of activity is a range that relates the volume of activity to the resources necessary to achieve that activity. For example, it may be decided that to produce up to 5000 plastic folders a certain cost structure is required, including the cost of people. If the company has a budget to produce 5000 folders in a specific time-frame, say a year, then irrespective of how many folders are produced during that period, so long as the total does not exceed 5000, it will be necessary to have in place the resources to produce 5000 folders. If it turns out that the business only produces 4000 folders, then the cost of producing those 4000 folders per unit is higher than the cost of producing 5000 units. I hope I haven't made a simple concept complex! Thus, we have an activity range of 0–5000.

At the low end of the range, the cost per unit is high and at the top end of the range the cost per unit is lower. Accordingly, operating at the top end of the range is clearly the best way to maximise profits. But there is a catch. At the bottom end of the range, resources are underutilised and when this happens, the resources are often applied in promoting the business to increase sales. Suddenly the business is at the top end of the range of activity and the CEO is happy and looking at the bottom line of the financial statements that indicate that profits are soaring.

The point is made in Chapters 15 and 16 on leadership and the Chapter 6 on "the theory of the organization" that there exists a close correlation between the extent of involvement of employees in the decision making process, providing feedback and productivity. So, when the financial statements are looking good and the business is at the top end of the activity range, the CEO ought to go down to the shop floor to ask people how they are going. The reason is that he or she will find something that doesn't show up on the financial statements. What will he or she find? Down there at the coal face everyone is at the limits of endurance.

The reasons for this is that even though, theoretically, the marginal cost is sufficient to meet the demand at the top of the activity range, the fact is that human beings are, believe it or not, just like you and me, or at least like me. When I am at the limits a number of things seem to happen. The first is that I make mistakes. The second is that I get cranky and upset people; the third is that I become less productive. The same phenomenon occurs in businesses. The reason is that humans are not mechanistic robots, and when they get to the top of the activity range they find that they aren't being as effective as they should be. Then what happens is that customers get upset and defect. Just ask Boeing![7]

This happens so frequently and is such a cause of businesses going into decline that I am spending so much time here stating the mathematically obvious. I am sure that everyone who has got this far will be saying "I know all this". Sure but just ask yourself whether you apply it to your business. If you don't keep an eye on marginal costs and manage them properly, you are headed for big trouble.

What we know is that while people might be under-utilised when activity is at the low end of the range, they become over utilised when activity gets to the top end of the range and management has to detect this before the business hits the wall and starts losing customers.

When activity gets to the top end of the range, there is a graph that looks like this:

There is no artificiality about the num-

Resources/ Work Base

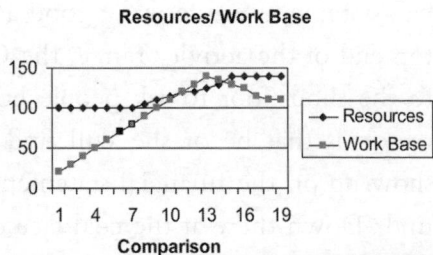

There is no artificiality about the numbers along the X axis because they represent the number of years a company has been in business and I have constructed this graph on the basis of experience with quite a few businesses over the years.

What happens when a business starts off is that it usually has a lot of resources but no customers. It then applies the resources to get the customers and for a while, everything is fine. The CEO looks at the financials and sees the profit booming but he or she gets a bit big for their boots and forgets to go down to the coal face and ask people how they are going. Sometimes, CEO's or owners tend to do silly things and drive down to a flash restaurant for a long lunch with their mates to tell them how good business is. They might even take their family for that six months tour that they felt they always deserved. In the meantime, Rome is burning and they don't know it because they haven't been down to the coal face for a while. Why should they? The financials say that the firm is on fire and, unfortunately, it often is, but not in the way the CFO sees it. The business is either bursting at the seams or has. Quite a few employees have left, putting more pressure on the remainder but any suggestion to the boss that they add staff is ignored because the profit is so good; let it keep going.

Regrettably, it doesn't keep going and when the boss comes back from overseas and finds quite a few people have left and sales are down, he or she gives everyone the rev up and tells them "so that is what happens the moment I turn my back". If only the boss understood the concept of marginal costs! It would also help if the CEO understood that costs are investments in competitive strategy and not an impact on profit.

If you look closely at the Resources graph you will note an interesting pattern forming around the year thirteen[8]. You will see that the Work Base graph forms a triangular pattern above the Resources graph. That triangle is an area that needs to be avoided at all costs in business and is known as "The Bermuda Triangle" where the demand of customers exceeds the capacity of the business to supply, resulting in disaffection and defection of customers. Management should constantly beware of the Bermuda Triangle.

Let us have a look and see what should have been done. No amount of financial accounting will reveal the stress levels in an organization. Financial statements only tell you what has happened in a financial sense and as these statements are history books, they are not terribly revealing as to what is actually happening at the moment.

However, if the CEO has an interest in Management Accounting and understands something about marginal costs, the order book should indicate where your marginal costs are in relation to demand. The reason is that when planning the need for staff to service the activity within the activity range, management would know what we have already demonstrated and that which is so obvious. At the low end of the activity range, the resources would be underutilised and at the upper end, people would be stretched to their limit. Accordingly, the order book compared with the activity range planned for the personnel establishment would tell at any one stage whether or not the business is at the limit of its marginal costs. Once management sees

---

8   For a description of the Bermuda Triangle see EW Sasser, PR Olsen & DD Wycoff, *Management of Service Operations: Cases and Readings*, Allyn and Bacon, Boston, 1978.

that the number of orders is getting towards the upper end of the projected range, it is the time to add resources, even though they might not be theoretically necessary to service current demand. However, if you don't service current demand with the same expedition as previously, customers will defect; something you want to avoid at all cost.

By way of example, suppose a business has put in place the resources to produce up to 5000 particular items over a twelve months period. If, after six months, orders have been received for 4,500 items the warning bells should be ringing that the business is under resourced and that the current resources will be stretched to the limit because they have had to produce in six months almost the entire year's production. If something isn't done quickly, the wheels are likely to fall off.

If resources are added as the orders get towards the high end of the activity range, then you are getting a picture like the beginning of the graph above. You have more resources than you have a customer base and so you then apply those resources to what you did previously which was to provide great service and go out and get more customers. If you leave it until too late, something quite unpleasant happens. Customers defect while you are desperately adding new resources and defecting customers tell other people about their bad experience and just as you are adding resources, your customer base is declining. Now, it is one thing to try and win back customers after you have upset them and another thing to go into the market for customers when you have a good reputation. If a business fails to manage its resources to be capable of effectively servicing and attract-ing customers, at some point in time it is in the situation of the business at the end period of the Resources/Work base graph on page 154.

If a business manages its marginal costs on the basis that they are investments in growth rather than an impact upon profits, management will know well before the stress threshold is set that it is necessary to move up to the next level of costs, even though initially, there may be under utilisation of resources. Otherwise, sixteen years or earlier down the track of a good business, management is back where it started except that it has a bad reputation and it is very difficult and expensive to come back from that situation. Once again, ask Boeing.

Being aware of this step-up syndrome and the necessity to maintain resources sufficient to more than adequately meet demand is much more easily accomplished if people understand this concept of marginal cost.

I would have to say, that on occasions, I have been called in to businesses that are financially in good shape and where the CEO doesn't know much about accounting but he does know a lot about the company and is in touch with the grassroots and the customers. I remember one case when a Managing Director of a construction company called me in to have a look at the company because he sensed that "there wasn't something quite right and I am having difficulty in getting the business to the next level". His timing was perfect because the problem was that the business was getting close to the danger point. That guy was not lucky. As Gary Player is oft quoted "The harder the practice, the luckier I get". He kept in touch with the business right down to the coal face.

MANAGEMENT ACCOUNTING II

Hopefully by now, readers will understand that the mathematics of Management Accounting that we have so far traversed are pretty simple and the principles demonstrated are rather obvious. In fact, they are so obvious that one wonders why we should waste time on covering the topic. The reason has to do with the comment my mother used to make whenever I went anywhere. "You would lose your head if it wasn't screwed on". The other day I looked high and low for my wristwatch and couldn't find it anywhere. The only place I didn't look was on my wrist. The number of times I have spent ages looking for my glasses only to find that I am wearing them is so embarrassing that I get terribly cross with myself for being so stupid.

We can work in a business every day of the week and on the weekends if we are crazy and there can be things staring us in the face, yet we don't notice them, not because we are stupid, but because we don't have disciplines in place to bring them to our attention. However, some times, we might have to dig a bit because a quick look at things is frequently insufficient to give us an accurate picture of what is going on. These great guys, Morse, Davis and Hartgraves who wrote the book on Management Accounting[1] draw attention to the risks involved in using average numbers and they provide a table of figures to demonstrate this danger of just using averages[2]. I am indebted to Professor's Hartgraves and Morse for permitting me to draw on the material contained in the fifth edition of their monumental work.

It is budget time and management looks at the financial and statistical information for the year just about to end and finds that the business has sold 500 units at an average cost of $11 per unit. They take that as the cost necessary to produce units sold. So, in budgeting they decide to adopt the cost of $11 per unit. Management then decides that on the basis of last year's figures the range for the coming year ought to be increased to 600 units and that the average cost will be $11.

Without management's knowledge, some young smart guy in accounts does another analysis of the current year's figures. He knew about a range of activity and the variability of costs if you look discretely within the range and so he constructs the following more discrete analysis of the current year's figures which identifies variability within the range. This analyst was aware of marginal costs and decides to break down the figures. It is known that the fixed costs amount to $3,000 and the variable cost is $5 per unit.

So, this is the table that the young analyst constructs[3].

---

1   There are other books on Management Accounting and the authors might take issue with this statement but I still think it is a great book.

2   We will look at this issue again when I explain the concept of a standard deviation at p. 241.

3   This is a straight lift out from *Management Accounting* ibid.

Customers	Total Cost	Average cost	Variable cost
100	3,500	35	5
200	4,000	20	5
300	4,500	15	5
400	5,000	12.5	5
500	5,500	11	5

What the young analyst identifies, by looking discretely at the costs at different levels within the range is that not surprisingly, the average cost varies according to the number of sales. He plucks up some courage and goes to management with his figures and says, "Hey, if you only sell 300 units this coming year instead of 600, the average cost per sale is going to be $15 and not $11 which is the average for the total sales in this current year". This sets a cat among the pigeons because the difference between $11 and $15 is the firm's margin. Management's response is "don't worry; based on last year's figures we will easily achieve the 500 and more likely the 600". So, they stay with the average cost of $11.

Bookshelves are overburdened with literature about budgeting and it can become an enormously complex undertaking. For current purposes, I want to introduce what I believe to be two approaches to budgeting that the management in this forgoing story might keep in mind before it proceeds hurriedly to dismiss the analysis of the young guy in accounts

The first approach is an historic approach. "We did such and such last year and so we should do such and such plus this year". So who says so? Death and taxes are a certainty as is the fact that the sun will predictably rise tomorrow in the East and set in the West at a predictable time, depending where you are in the world. Otherwise, the future is uncertain and cannot be predicted simply by looking at the past. A lot of people got caught in the financial meltdown in 2008. The reason being that they thought the world would never come to an end and the good times would keep rolling along. Well, there were quite a few gurus[4] who said that the good times were over and not too many people paid attention. Some of them went broke but a lot of them sent others broke while walking away themselves with a pocket full of money from what is euphemistically called "commissions".

Budgeting is perhaps the second most difficult aspect of management. The most difficult aspect is making budget. However, making budget is a little easier if instead of using the historic approach, management use what I call a "dynamic" approach. This is a bit more difficult because it necessitates looking forward and contemplating the likelihood of different scenarios emerging in the course of the budget period.

Here, Management Accounting can be of some assistance because while it will call on past data, it can do so in discrete segments so that discrete trends can be identified rather than an overall picture. For instance, suppose a business sells 903 units in the previous year. There might be a tendency to say "well, that is the benchmark and in relation to that benchmark we will have to allow for variable and fixed costs of such and such because we are likely to do a

---

4   Gary Shilling of A. Gary Shilling & Co, a financial advisory firm and Professor Nouriel Roubini, Professor of Economics at New York University both forecast the financial meltdown with extraordinary accuracy. In addition, my dear friend, Professor Sunil Erevelles (Belk School, Charlotte NC).

little better this year and so it is safe to add some costs to cover the increased activity". However, the young guy in accounts, not to be deterred, comes along and says that it is necessary to look more closely at the figures and this is what is found:

Jan	Feb	Mar	Apr	May	June	July	Aug	Sep	Oct	Nov	Dec	
60	70	80	80	85	90	88	85	70	70	65	60	903

Average 75.25

Aug/Dec 350
Average 70

The irrepressible young whiz kid points out that while the average over the year is 75.25 units a month, in fact, if you look at a discrete segment being the last five months, the average units sold is only 70 and this multiplied by twelve equals 840 which is a lot less than was sold last year[5].

Management is not too keen on the Whiz kid pocking his nose into the accounts and so they go back a year earlier and dig out the figures of sales for that earlier year and they find that in the last quarter of that year, sales went through the roof. So, they say to the whiz kid "look, the figures

5   While these figures are fictitious, they are based on an experience I had when I was asked to advice some guys who wanted to acquire a business. The financials indicated that the company was in good shape. However, I was concerned that the founding owner of the business had recently died and so I got details of the sales since his death and found to my horror that the sales had fallen off dramatically in those few months. Because the fall off was recent, it didn't show up in the financials (remember the story about accrued accounting?). However, the discrete evidence was compelling and I pointed this out to the guys who nevertheless proceeded with the acquisition. They believed the recent trend was an aberration but found to their misfortune that it was systemic.

for last August to December are aberrational. In previous years, August to December have been our best months. We will certainly increase sales this year so we will beef up our budget by 10% on last year's average".

In fact, warning bells should be ringing in management's ears.

There is a clear sign that something is wrong. If sales in the last five months of the year just gone have dropped off when the sales for the same period for the previous year were up, there has to be an explanation for the difference. There may be a number of explanations but the first one to look at is whether the marginal costs were sufficient to support the growth that had been experienced in the previous year.

Then of course, it is necessary to look at the economy and see what is happening there and then to get a handle on the industry to see what is happening there so that you can start to re-evaluate your predictions for future activity. The next thing that should be done, if it hasn't already been done, is talk to customers to get a handle on why they aren't buying. There is frequently a tendency on the part of management when it gets negative feedback from employees or customers to bury their heads in the sand and ignore the data on the basis that customers and employees don't know what they are talking about.[6] (Never bury your head in the sand or be frightened in the face of evidence to admit that you are wrong). All of that research will give an indication to the late trend so that you will hopefully be able to adopt remedial action and plan in the budget accordingly,

---

6   GM might not be in the trouble today, if they had taken a leaf out of Toyota's book and built their business model around market and employee feedback.

not just from the point of view of revenue, but also from the point of view of what costs are necessary to right the ship. The last thing you want to discover is that you are in the Bermuda Triangle.

Strangely enough, if, on looking at the figures it seems that the trend is upwards, exactly the same investigations should be conducted. It may be that you are getting into the no-no zone of the work exceeding the resources and you will learn to react quickly before much damage is done. You should always be in touch with the staff at the coal face; talking to your customers and keeping in touch with the industry and an eye on competitors as well as economic trends. In this way it is possible to minimise the risks of budget miscalculations. In addition, today's businesses are caught up, whether one likes it or not, in global economic activity that continually sends ripples throughout the world and can have impacts even on the food store servicing multi-storied officers vacated by failed bankers.

All of these factors and more need to be taken into account in budgeting. One of the quotes that I bring to the attention of my clients is from a friend of mine[7]

"The future arrives just a little sooner than we expect."

However, reliance on trends and discrete information within the organization's armoury of data are often very revealing and tell a different story to the final year's accounts because, after all, the financial statements are history books whereas businesses are about the future.

There are quite a few tricks to learn about Management

7   Professor Sunil Erevelles, Associate Professor of Marketing at the Belk School of Management, University of North Carolina.

Accounting and before a business gets too big, an effort ought to be made to get a handle on the subject. Quite a few Universities conduct courses on financial analysis for non-financial executives. Stanford, where I did an advanced management course, has such a programme but I am sure there are many universities that conduct similar courses around the world. Some may be on line. Working through the text of *Management Accounting* by Professors Morse, Davis and Hartgraves wouldn't hurt one bit.

One final aspect of Management Accounting that interests me as an ex-lawyer and current management consultant is its application to the practice of law.

In this context I want to revisit the concept of variable cost as against fixed costs. There are some businesses that mistake variable cost for fixed costs. For instance, a legal practice, given a certain range of activity, will require a basic level of personnel and equipment to produce an outcome for the client. It will not be using raw materials or other supplies for cases but most of the costs will simply be in-house. Accordingly, in a broad sense, all of the costs will be fixed. Having stated the obvious so frequently I am a little embarrassed to do it again but because I have noticed in legal practices a disinclination to take on board some of these basic concepts of Management Accounting, I will restate the obvious. In a legal practice, operating within a range of activity, most if not all costs in the practice will be fixed, which means that if the practice operates at the low end of the range, the cost per unit (law case) will be higher than if it is operating at the top end of the range. Accordingly, throughput becomes critical if costs are to be contained and the client is to get the benefit of efficiencies.

That is not how it happens in many legal practices that bill clients for hours worked rather than work done. By that I mean that irrespective of the state of the case, whether it is complete or not, bills go out on a monthly basis for the hours worked. In that sense, the range of activity becomes the number of hours worked instead of the number of cases completed. In fact, the "charge out rate", as it is called, is a rate fixed at the beginning of the financial year in budget time based upon what costs are expected to be incurred by the firm plus an added margin. In that sense, a law firm which generates its billings by billable hours based upon anticipated costs and margins, can never pass on to the customer the benefit of leveraging fixed costs by spreading it across the number of cases completed. It wouldn't matter how many cases are completed, the number of hours billed determines the revenue. In this scenario, the range of activity becomes hours worked rather than benefits sold. In budgeting, billable hours become the activity of the law firm and the driver of revenue. This deprives the law firm and its clients of the benefits of efficiency. The reason is that whether or not the budgeted billable hours are achieved, the cost to the customer will not alter. The customer will still be billed for the number of hours worked. If, on the other hand, the law firm charged a fixed fee per client matter, the cost to the client would reduce according to the number of cases that are completed within the time-frame and this reduced cost could go partly to the client and partly to the profits of the law firm.

While my earlier profession was that of a lawyer, I never could, when practising, and still can't, as a management consultant, accept that an hour is a benefit.

LEADERSHIP

There are libraries full of books on leadership, in addition to an almost unlimited number of academic programmes. Everyone has a view about leadership and as many people agree with one another as they differ. However, in my experience there are some unaltering aspects that are frequently forgotten in the discussions.

The first is that leadership is inextricably involved with the organization and without understanding the theory of the organization, it is not possible to properly understand the function of leadership.

The second is that by and large, in a general sense, people are largely predictable in their behaviour but despite that, management is frequently successful beyond imagination in alienating the people upon whom they rely to achieve their objectives.

The third is that the internal elements of the organization of the business are only a part of the organization with which a leader should be concerned because the internal organization is linked on the one hand with the suppliers and would be suppliers to the organization and with the wider community, called "the market", on the other hand. Within this chain, there are manifold functions that affect the end benefit to the consumer and to the extent that this chain doesn't work as well as it should, the consumer will suffer, as will the business.

The fourth is that all organizations are what might be called "societal" entities in that they are made up of people who come together as a community to achieve certain objectives. Ideally, they come together to achieve the objectives of the organisation but this is where leadership becomes tricky which leads us to the fifth important aspect. However, before we move to the fifth aspect, it is important to mention that this fourth factor involves the necessity to state the negative which is that organizations and the people working in them are not mechanistic instruments but a collection of unique variable human creatures who do not respond well to expectations that they perform as mechanisms. Many managers would be horrified to think that their subordinates consider that they are mechanistic tools in a machine called the "organization" that has as its sole purpose the attainment of financial objectives. In *The Principles of Scientific Management*[1] Frederick Winslow Taylor introduced the concept of "the competent man" and reduced the equation of one of scientific measurement which spooned the underlying thesis of management which has persisted to this day and which has as its central characteristic the statistical measurement of output (KPI) as the basis of evaluating the human contribution to enterprise.

The fifth aspect has been identified time and again by

1   FW Taylor, *The Principles of Scientific Management,* Elibron Classics, 1911.

some of the earlier writers on the subject and it is to do with the fact that all people working within an organization have needs and to the extent that those needs are not met, the organization suffers as do its customers. It could be put more forcibly the other way around. If the needs of the employees of an organization are not met to a satisfactory degree, the customer suffers as does the business.

A sixth aspect is that authority can be either conferred from above or earned from below. Conferred authority is that which occurs when a person is appointed to a leadership position by superiors and has little value. Earned authority is that which is surrendered to the leader by the people who are to be led and effective leadership is impossible without the leader having earned this authority by generating a degree of trust and respect that is so essential to enjoying the wholehearted support of those who are to be led[2].

We learnt earlier that the revenue of an organization is directly proportional to the benefits it confers on its customers. The greater the benefits perceived by the customer for the price, the greater the revenue. We also learnt that benefits are intended to satisfy the needs of the customer. It is the same within the organization. People working in organizations have needs and to the extent that the organization can satisfy those needs, the employee will respond as does a satisfied customer: with loyalty, that in the case of the customer, creates goodwill and in the case of the

---

2   A study of the exploration expeditions of Sir Ernest Shackleton will be richly rewarded by creating a deep understanding of this concept of earned authority and what can be achieved by generating a level of trust among those who are to be led that they literally trusted Shackleton with their lives. Their trust was rewarded by one of the most remarkable stories of leadership in history. The story is told by Shackleton himself in *The Polar Journeys*, The Collins Press, 2002.

employee; a willingness to return to the job with ever increasing enthusiasm.

The next aspect which I believe to be an important quality of a leader is that he or she has the courage of their convictions. In my early days as a lawyer, I gave some ambivalent advice to my boss (which is not an unusual tactic of the lawyer because it enables the lawyer to have a bet each way and thus claim, irrespective of the outcome, that they were right). He read the advice and then leaned back in his chair and said "I would sooner a wrong no than a vacillating yes". In the end, the leader has to make the decision and put his or her neck on the line. Generally, the decision will relate to something that is to happen or not happen in the future. As we know, people such as analysts who try to forecast the future have a pretty bad track record. So, the leader is making decisions about the future in the knowledge that, at best, uncertainty will be associated with the decision. More often than not, the executive who makes decisions without consultation will get it wrong. Decision making cannot be divorced from the other functions of a leader and particularly that of staying in touch with the views, values, experience and beliefs of others in the organization. It is more likely, that if the Leader is aware of this wealth of material, decisions will be more likely to be successful and almost certain to be supported. However, at some point the leader has to make the call. The hesitant leader, who defers decisions and puts off difficult issues, will lose the support of his or her followers. It takes guts coupled with sensitivity to the views of others to be a leader.

This brings me to the final aspect I consider important and that relates to this issue of needs. What are the needs of the people working in the modern organization? Without directly mentioning him, a number of writers[3] introduce the concept of Maslow's hierarchy of needs.[4]

At a basic level, McGregor[5] points out that financial remuneration is intended to satisfy the needs of employees that exist outside of the organization. They don't and can't spend their salary within the organization. They satisfy their needs in relation to money outside of the organization. What Drucker, McGregor and in a much more profound way; Roethlisberger[6] and Barnard[7], identify as the need which exist within the organization is the need for individuals to have their uniqueness addressed by way of recognition of their status as important individuals and to be treated with dignity.

In a sense, all of these aspects can perhaps be restated in a broad description of the important aspects of leadership, but it might be better to separate this description and classify it as a sixth aspect. Chris Argyris has identified organizations as having knowledge which is made up of the continuum of the various stories and experiences of the people working in that organization and as a result, the organization consists of many individual stories and experiences. The ability of a leader to recognise this and that all wisdom does not lie in the mind of the leader but much of it is to be found in the minds of the individuals within the organization has an enormous influence on successful leadership. As against

---

3   Particularly McGregor, Drucker (in his earliest writings) and Barnard.

4   See AH Maslow, *Motivation and Personality,* 2nd edn, Harper & Row, 1970.

5   Prof D McGregor, *The Human Side of Enterprise*, McGraw Hill, 1985.

6   Roethlisberger & Dixon, *Management and the Worker*, HUP, 1939.

7   Chester I Barnard, *The Functions of the Executive*, 30th edn, HUP.

that, the leaders who shut themselves off from these stories and wisdom become intellectually and emotionally ostracised from the community of employees in that organization. Having the ability to tune in and listen to that wealth of knowledge, emotions and experience and to respond to it enables the leader to become part of the organization rather than a remote and ineffectual controller.

I have run quite a few organizations and I am not sure to what extent people have regarded me as a good, bad or indifferent leader, but I do know that the moment I ignored one of these aspects I would find myself in trouble. Perhaps my failure to constantly be aware of these two last aspects gave rise to the greatest difficulties. In practical terms, the widespread failure of leaders at any level to recognise that people respond to compliments is dumbfounding.

Putting all these things together, leadership requires a constant awareness of the needs of the people within the wider organization of the suppliers, internal operations and customers so that these needs can be addressed, be they a need for more resources such as technology or money, a need for more help in the way of additional staff, a need for a change in direction or simply a need for recognition as individuals and to be treated with dignity.

Perhaps I can illustrate this last issue with a little story. There was (and still is) a very successful construction company that used a lot of sub-contractors (suppliers). It had developed the practice, because of the initiative of someone in finance, to delay payment to sub-contractors well beyond trading time frames and investing the money on the short term money market. The company could not understand why it was often non-competitive in tenders. In getting around speaking to the suppliers I picked up a huge degree of anger because the contractors thought that they were doing a great job (which they were) but their efforts, often beyond the call of duty, were not recognised by the construction company, which was so slow in payment. The contractors knew what was happening to the money and were angry because they felt they were being treated with contempt. The recurrent term used by sub-contractors to describe the contractor was "arrogance". What they were wanting more than the money, was respect; that old thing of status and dignity.

The senior management of the construction company was completely unaware of this situation. Once the job was done, they went on to the new job and the issue of payment was left to the administrator and finance people.

The end of the story was that when these contractors were asked to give a price to the construction company on a new job, they were invariably approached for a price by the construction company's competitors, some of whom paid on the knocker. So, guess who got the better price and were placed in a more competitive situation? You bet; the competitors!

A pat on the back goes a lot further than a kick in the pants. I am amazed at the consistency with which people in different organizations complain that they always know when they have done something wrong because they get a kick in the pants but they never know when they do something right.

However, there is a balance and just as it is necessary for a leader to be aware of the stories, experience and wisdom of the employees and to respond both individually and collectively to that knowledge, it does not mean that the leader should surrender his or her leadership. One quality of a leader is the ability to weigh up the views of his or her staff in the context of the leader's own wisdom and experience with the result that the leader may sometimes disagree with the employees.

I can remember being called in to salvage a huge resort that had been built by the Japanese in the nineties when money was being handed out in Japan like confetti. This consortium had ploughed money into the establishment of this resort which included a golf club. The golf club had become quite famous and enjoyed national and international support. However, it and the property section of the resort were in deep financial crisis and neither the property section nor the golf club had ever made a profit. Fortunately, concurrent with my appointment, the General Manager of the golf club had departed and that section, which contained multiple sub-sections such as catering, functions, retail etc., was staggering along under the leadership of a headless chook. On speaking on a confidential basis with the staff of the golf club I found on the one hand a degree of frustration at the direction of the club and on the other, a great deal of knowledge and energy to do something about it that hitherto had been ignored. I appointed a management team from this group and told them that they knew a lot more about running a golf club than me and I had other fish to fry so I would leave it up to them. I would never be critical if anything they did turned out badly, but I would be cross if they did nothing. All I could do was to find resources for them if that is what they wanted.

So, I attended weekly management meetings and at one

meeting they said they had come up with a great idea. They said that the price of a round of golf was too expensive and they said that they wanted to reduce the price. I immediately recoiled from this idea because it had taken so much effort to achieve the status and branding of the course that to now reduce the price might result in a downgrading of the perception of the market as to the status of the course[8]. I said that I was uneasy about that proposal. The committee responded by saying that I had left it up to them to make decisions and I wouldn't criticise them if they made a mistake. After explaining my concerns I said "Sure", "but I didn't cut myself out of the deal. Why don't you think about it for a week and we will look at it again next week". The following week, the committee said that they had a better idea. The proposal this time was to have a standby rate which was the same price as the existing rate provided that if people phoned before 8 am on the day, and there were spaces available, one person paying the full rate could bring along a guest for nothing. So, there is the wisdom of the masses, which would never have surfaced had those guys not been given the opportunity to be heard.

The management committee did a lot of other things that had never been done under the previous management and as a result, within three months, the club made its first profit in history.

The only credit that I claim for this success is that I got to know these guys and decided that they knew a hell of a lot more than I did about running a golf club and so I

---

8   Apart from that I believe that price wars are destructive and result in everyone reducing prices to the point where the market share remains the same but the price of the product is less.

trusted them to take initiatives knowing that they would be supported. That job was quite interesting because, when I arrived on the scene, all the staff were missing two week's wages because the previous owners had left with no cash in the tin. It was going to take some time before I could recover those wages from the administrator, yet, despite that, all these people worked way beyond the call of duty just to make the club work and never raised the question of salary[9]. I mention this in order to dispel the current "wisdom" that wages and incentive payments fixed according to certain KPIs are the factors that drive productivity and human commitment. Financial incentives are great for inducing crooks to take risks with other people's money but recognition of the worth of the individual and of each person's dignity is a far more fundamental need that is hugely unsatisfied in today's corporations.

After this, the discussion on leadership becomes quite tricky. However; there are two issues that are constantly visited by commentators. The first is the age old question of whether leaders are born or made. I believe that there is no point in asking the question because no one knows the answer. What we do know is that different people with different personalities, competencies and styles have been successful leaders.

One point that seems to get ignored in this discussion is the fact that each individual is unique. In fact, this is perhaps the most ignored and yet demonstrably valid factor in the entire burgeoning discussion of management. Let me make a statement that I claim to be undeniably and

---

9   I actually raised it frequently by reporting to them on the status of the negotiations with the Administrator.

incontrovertibly true. There is and only ever will be one
Steve Jobs or one Bill Gates or one Warren Buffett. And
yet, business schools and management journals and maga-
zines study these guys as though you will find in them the
philosopher's stone that magically enables us to be a Bill
Gates or a Steve Jobs or a Warren Buffet. Baloney! What
we have to continually treasure is our uniqueness so that we
can become more and more ourselves rather than an image
of someone else or a symbol that fits into the management
jigsaw so that we try to be what the corporation wants us
to be rather than being ourselves. That is not to say that
we can't learn lessons. Indeed, the ability to relate what we
learn to our personal situation is one of the skills of leaders.
One of the most valuable learning techniques is to evaluate
criticism. Frequently, people in authority respond badly to
criticism with one of two responses. One is that they agree
with the substance of the criticism but respond by saying
"That doesn't apply to me" or they simply disagree and say
that the critic is wrong.

An example of the first situation occurs when I say that
there has to be an opportunity for staff to provide feedback
to management in circumstances where staff feels comfortable about providing that feedback. The frequent response
is "Oh, we have plenty of forums for that to happen. For
instance, once a month we sit down with the staff in a staff
meeting and tell them that everything is on the table. We
have annual performance reviews where staff are free to
provide feedback and we leave a suggestion box in the staff
dining room." When I get this line I ask management how
successful is the process in generating feedback. "Well, you
know, we often think it is a waste of time because staff just

sit around waiting for someone else to say something with the result that we wouldn't get anything out of it unless we stimulate the discussion with our own input. We rarely get suggestions in the suggestion box and it is even rarer for staff to provide feedback to us in performance reviews. So, we are pretty happy that if there was something we needed to know it would come out."

I have interviewed employees on a confidential basis and invariably, people in this environment, have a litany of concerns. Sometimes I have arrived late for an interview with a member of the staff and there might be a woman waiting to be interviewed and I can immediately identify that there is something wrong because she has a red rash on her neck. We go in and after pleasantries and breaking the ice and gaining the person's confidence, the whole sad story of the organization from that person's perspective emerge in tears. "Why haven't you raised these issues in the staff meetings or in your performance review?" The response invariably is "are you mad or something? What do you think management would say or do if I started to tell them what I thought of them? I need my job for God's sake". These are the very organizations where management is saying they are listening to their people. In fact, the opposite is happening. They are closing the door to their people and losing access to one of the great resources of an organization. Issues become, as Argyris[10] says "un-discussable".

A successful leader has to be able to generate sufficient trust within the band of followers so that they feel free to come and speak their mind whether what they have to say is criticism, the conveying of bad news or suggestions for

---

10 A Wesley, 'Organizational learning II', 1996.

improvement. The more people feel uneasy about approaching management along these lines, the less effective is management and leadership. By distancing themselves from the views, knowledge and opinions of employees, management sets up a barrier that results in the unheard employees forming one of these informal organizations that operates without the knowledge of management.

The second phenomenon that acts as a break on effective leadership is the state of denial which is usually associated with arrogance of which; sadly, there are too many examples in corporate culture[11]. Perhaps one of the more dramatic examples of this is the story of Peter Drucker's involvement with GM. During and immediately after the war, Drucker had an intimate involvement with GM, which enabled him to speak to many people and form views as to the effectiveness of management and the direction of the company. He then wrote a book called *The Concept of the Corporation*[12] in which he gave credit to GM for taking a lot of ground breaking initiatives such as introducing the concept of decentralisation into the work place. However, the book did contain observations that suggested there were areas of opportunities for GM to make changes or do things differently. When the book was published, it was criticised heavily by the management of GM and it was banned within the organization. Attempts were made to belittle the book and its observations.

Despite this, other organizations such as Ford Motor Company and the Catholic diocese of New York adopted it and used Drucker's concepts and observations to restruc-

---

11 See for instance my discussion about Boeing in Chapter 8.

12 P Drucker, *The Concept of the Corporation*, John Day Company, 1946.

ture their organizations. General Motors was in denial and refused to listen to criticism, no matter how pleasantly presented and just kept going its own way without change. They ignored the wisdom of the masses which was conveyed to them by medium of Drucker's book. When an organization completely loses touch with the emotive and intellectual state of mind of the people lower in the organization, trouble lies ahead. As we know, GM, convinced of the sanctity of its own business model and organizational structures, ploughed steadfastly ahead to carnage and bankruptcy[13].

The other issue frequently raised and in relation to which there would appear to be extensive academic agreement coupled with apparent anecdotal experience, is that there is a need for different types of leaders in different situations. Churchill is often quoted as an example of this in that he was very successful in war time in bringing the nation together against its greatest threat in history and yet, post-war, he was rejected by the electorate. I may be wrong but I am not sure Churchill could really be looked upon as a great leader in the true categorisation of that term. Churchill had a deep sense of the British traditions and was able to translate that into oratory of such emotive force that there is little parallel in history, save of course for Shakespeare's creation of Henry V (*we few, we happy few…*). Indeed, when you listen to replays of Churchill's famous speeches, you can almost hear Shakespeare prompting him as a speech writer. His oratory stirred and welded a nation and prepared every man, woman and child in England for the ultimate fate, sending a warning to Hitler that inva-

---

13 See article by Alex Taylor in *Fortune*, December 8 2008.

sion would not achieve victory. In fact, they were hollow words expressed more in hope than expectation because at the same time, the British diplomatic service was actively knocking on the door of Roosevelt to come to the aid of Britain. If Roosevelt had turned a deaf ear to those calls, it would have been interesting to see just how Churchill would have been judged by history. In the end, it was the presence of American troops that turned the tide of the European war.

Another more contemporary example is that of the Italian Manager who turned around the Italian conglomerate, ENI. His story is recorded in the summary of an interview in the *Harvard Business Review*[14]. It is well worth reading. However, its relevance to this discussion is that for some time, Franco Bernabe, had been side-lined by senior management at ENI, mainly because he didn't go along with the existing culture of graft and corruption in which senior management were feathering their nest. Out of the blue he was appointed by the Board as CEO to turn the organization around.

The entire organisation was hopelessly corrupted and the Italian government wanted someone from outside the current management clique to take the hard decisions in order to shift the direction of the company. Because he had been side-lined by the existing management, he had been able to connect with the rank and file and earn their respect. When he was appointed CEO, he knew precisely what was wrong with the organization and what needed to be done to fix it. He was extremely successful and demonstrated his qualities of leadership principally, by responding to the concerns of

14 See *HBR* July/August 1998 pp. 81-94.

the many in the organization whose values he respected and by having the courage of his convictions. When the rank and file saw him taking the initiatives that they felt were so desperately needed in the company while turning his back on the egregious behaviour of the former executives, he had won the rank and file and earned leadership.

He was later appointed as CEO of Telecom Italia which was taken over by Olivetti in 1999. In an article in the *Harvard Business Review*[15] the author was at pains to point out that different situations required different types of leaders and in this particular case, Bernabe was not suited to the position because it required someone with merger and acquisition knowledge and he stepped down after six months in the job. I am far from certain that this illustration demonstrates the author's argument that different types of situations define the specific nature of leadership. Bernabe's decision to step aside was an act of a leader who saw that the company was going in a direction different to that with which he was comfortable and decided to let the takeover company (Olivetti) go down that route. It is interesting that some years later, Bernabe was approached by the Board of Telecom Italia to become Chairman.

It may be that different situations require different types of leaders and that the qualifications one leader has for a particular job might disqualify that person from undertaking another and different assignment. We also have to keep in mind some differences. For instance, the term "management" is not interchangeable with "leadership". There is also a difference between the role of a CEO and an

---

15 C Fernández-Aráoz, 'Hiring without firing', *Harvard Business Review*, July-August 1999, pp. 109-110.

operations manager.

Many people were surprised at the appointment of a former Boeing executive to become the CEO of Ford Motor company. Alan Mulally had worked with Boeing for thirty-seven years and people questioned whether someone who had no experience in the auto industry could do the job. It is interesting that when the financial crisis struck in the USA in 2008, Ford was the only American auto manufacturer that didn't have to go to the government for a handout and quickly moved to profitability.

Leadership in its truest sense involves the establishment of an element of such trust between the leader and his or her followers that the followers will give deep intellectual and emotional commitment to the objectives of the organization. However, building that trust involves the patient engagement of the leader with an extensive cross section of the organization so that the leader tunes into this "informal organization" and is aware of the currents and cross currents that need to be negotiated. In the end, the leader has to establish some form of understanding that the objectives of the organization are not only well known to the employees but also represent the values of the employees and their personal need for recognition as being important in the journey. Without that relationship the leader will find it difficult to bring subordinates willingly along for the ride.

In its simplest form, leadership involves having followers; something which is so often forgotten. This once again introduces the competing views of people in the workplace as mechanistic items carrying out the direction of management, as against that of the individual whose aspirations are acknowledged by management and are included in the

186 THE 6-HOUR MBA

direction of the enterprise according to shared values and a shared vision that confers societal benefits.

I look upon the first aspect of leadership as "conferred" Someone has appointed a leader and this creates an expectation in an organization that the leader has authority by virtue of the appointment to the position. Orders and directions are given by virtue of that authority.

As indicated previously[16] I believe that broadly speaking, there are two types of leadership. The first type is what I call "conferred" leadership when a person has been appointed to a position of leadership by some higher authority such as a Board. At the time of appointment, the appointee merely has conferred authority which is the authority to give directions by virtue of the appointment. Leaders who rely on this "conferred" authority tend to assume that they have to be the fountain of all wisdom.

The other type of leadership is what I call "earned" authority and that is authority earned by gaining the respect of those who are to be led. Without that authority, it is inevitable that those people who withhold their respect for the leader will form into an informal organization that will be at odds with the aims of the so called leader. Earned authority is the only authority that can ever be effective. The leaders of ENI who preceded Barnabe only had conferred authority whereas Barnabe earned his authority and was therefore effectual.

There is the argument that the leader has to be a visionary and, to a certain extent that is true but it is no more true than saying that it is desirable that everyone has a vision. What gets constantly forgotten in today's corporate world

---

16 See p. 171.

is that organizations are made up of more than a CEO[17]. As McGregor repeatedly points out, in any organization; there is a need for equilibrium in the interdependency of relationships. A CEO can do no more than permitted by the resources at her or his disposal and is therefore dependent upon the employees of the organization.

Steve Jobs is clearly a brilliant entrepreneur, but it is inconceivable that he invented the i-pod by himself. Even if he was the person who suddenly developed the idea (and the recurrent experiences of great discoveries being made contemporaneously by different people in different locations would suggest that he was not the only person to come up with the idea), the fact is that he had to develop the support of the people at Apple to convert that vision into a technical reality. It is in that area that his true genius of leadership was brought to bear.

As against that, I have been in many organizations in which I have interviewed the staff and have found many of them to have great vision and most of my successes have been a result of listening to them and using whatever my skills are in bringing their vision to reality. It is that trick of making things happen that characterises the leader. The most successful leaders have been those who understand the interdependency of the relationships in an organization and that the leader is just as dependent if not more so on the subordinates as they are on the leader.

Might I finish this chapter with the sad reflection that in almost all crisis cases in which I have been involved, after interviewing the people in the organization, I have discovered that the employees know what is wrong, they

17 See the discussion in Chapter 6 *Theory of the Organization*.

know what needs to be done but have never had the power or authority to do anything about the problem. What is so sad is that within the organization, all the knowledge to address problems is there but can't be accessed because of the disenfranchisement of the employees in that critical area. Accordingly, an informal organization that contains that knowledge, forms and actually insulates that knowledge from management. It is almost like a doctor seeing a patient dying and knowing what has to be done to save the life, but no one will give the doctor permission to do what has to be done. That is the greatest failure of leaders and it is, as I said, so sad.

One exception in my experience was a company which was really well run and which involved the staff in just about every initiative. However, in costing its projects, it relied on a person called an "estimator". The CEO couldn't understand why the cash flow was deteriorating so fast and even called in high status accountants who didn't pin point the problem. By the time I came in, I discovered that the estimator was just estimating the price of each job without taking into account back office and support costs, which were substantial with the result that each job was being completed at a loss. I had to advise the owners to put the business in administration. This experience did suggest to me that any leader of a corporation has to understand the subtle financial issues involved or have someone such as a CFO who does understand these issues and makes sure that the financial thing doesn't go pear shaped.

Some years ago I undertook the laborious task of going through all the Harvard Business Review articles on leadership over the past ten years and made a summary of the characteristics that emerged from those articles as being important to successful leadership. Five broad categories of behaviour emerged as relevant in assessing leadership performance.

The first category was "Operational" which relates to the effectiveness of the person to actually undertake functional tasks such as seeing through on a project and making sure things happen.

The second category involves the ability of the leader to relate effectively with those under the leader's control.

The third category involves the personal qualities of the leader.

The fourth category is a miss-match of miscellaneous factors and the final category relates to behaviour of the leader that is looked upon negatively by those under the leader's control.

Following is the table that summarises these various characteristics.

Operational	People	Self	Miscellaneous	Negative
Follow through on vision X 3	Feed back from staff X 9	Humility X 5	Questioning rules X 2	Control Freak X 2
Detailed planning	Develop a shared vision X 3	Self awareness X 4	Informal organizations X 2	
Involvement in recruiting	Mutual respect X 2	Political skills X 3	Transfer responsibility to Units	
	Emotional intelligence X 2	Calm in a crisis X 2	Motivation	
	Building trust	Authentic	Reward according to performance	
	Empathy			
	Team orientations			
	Respect for people			
	Uniqueness of individual			
	Concentrate on people's strengths			
	Courage of staff to tell the boss			

I find it quite interesting that by far the most recurrent qualities fall into the "People" category and in that
category, feedback from staff recurs more than any other
single characteristic. The next most recurrent characteristic
is "Humility".

LEADERSHIP II

One evening, I took time off from writing this book to have a quick meal in a Thai café. After a quick meal, a young woman who had waited on me presented me with the modest account and a fortune cookie. I don't know why, but I never open fortune cookies but for some reason I did on this occasion. There, shouting out to me from this miniscule piece of paper was the message "It takes more than a good memory to make good memories" I suddenly thought of all of the frustrations that had been expressed to me over the years by people in the workplace. I thought of Boeing, with the constant friction between management and the worker and I thought of the millions of layoffs that had been experienced by the American worker as a result of the financial crisis (or so it was said). When I read this fortune cookie I just wondered how many people with good memories had been provided by their bosses with good memories of their working experiences.

I know nothing about psychology although I have read a bit of Maslow[1] to whom reference has been made earlier

---

1   AH Maslow, *Motivation and Personality*, 2nd edn, Harper & Row, 1970.

and in particular in Chapter 7. However, I have interviewed thousands of people in the workplace over the past twenty or so years and the dominant theme of almost all of those interviews was one of frustration about the inability of the people to influence the direction of the business on the one hand and the determination of the boss on the other, to go in a direction that the staff considered unwise and unproductive.

There are many well-run companies but as against that, my experience, academic literature and business periodicals recount case after case where management is estranged from the staff. Despite this, businesses get by and many make serious money but, as we saw in Chapter 7, the productive potential of many businesses is frustrated. It is likely that the level of frustration across organizations throughout the world is of such a dimension as to constitute an enormous impediment to world productivity

However, the issue that often interests me when I go into a business or read about a business is the frequency with which Boards of Directors have difficulties with managers and particularly CEO's. When I read about corporate America I can see this phenomenon being repeated in the smaller organizations with which I have been involved. It is the lack of alignment between the objectives of management and the expectations of staff, that often result in a bemusement and frustration on the part of the staff.

As we discovered in the previous chapter, one phenomenon that exists in every organization is the unfulfilled expectation held by employees that their needs will be satisfied and frequently those needs are other than money. This is frequently associated with decision making that results in direction to staff rather than consultation. The staff is expected to do what they are told[2].

I have pondered at length over this phenomenon and gradually I came to the conclusion, without any serious empirical evidence, that a huge percentage of the population have, to different degrees, a sense of insecurity and a certain lack of self-esteem. This manifests itself in the organization in different ways. A lot of people have so little confidence in themselves that they readily defer to others in the belief that they, themselves, can't possibly be right. Even when what the boss says doesn't make sense, there is a tendency for people to conclude that the boss must know what she or he is talking about. What they don't realise is that it is quite possible and statistically likely that the boss also has some sense of insecurity and lack of self-esteem and consequently has doubts about his or her decision but would feel that it discloses a weakness if they appeared less than authoritative and confident. This sense of authority further weakens the resolve of others with a sense of insecurity and so they just go along with the decision.

This is where the thing gets interesting because there are just straws in the wind in the literature that suggests others might have a similar view[3]. We explained McGregor's theory X and theory Y in the Chapter 6[4] but for now, we can inaccurately summarise theory X as the dominant

---

2   This characteristic of management was described in Chapter 6 according to McGregor's theory X.

3   For instance, see the works of Dan Goleman, *Emotional Intelligence*; Marcus Buckingham, *First Break all the Rules* and that of Professor Jeffrey Sonenfeld at Yale, particularly in relation to the Hawthorne experiments.

4   Prof D McGregor, *The Human Side of Enterprise*, 25th edn, McGraw Hill, 1985, pp. 39–40.

managerial theory today because it equates work done for money paid. You do so much work and I will pay you so much money[5]. McGregor says:

> *"The upper-level management who holds Theory X can usually accept the idea of delegation, but when he puts it into action he is faced with a loss of the control on which his whole conception of management is based."*[6]

Later, McGregor makes the point that managers have what he calls a downward dependency. In other words, they are dependent for the results that they want to achieve on the performance of their subordinates. He does concede that some managers are aware of the importance of that dependency. However, he goes on and says:

> *"Others, who do not recognise this downward dependence (and these are the majority), are more concerned with their own performance and their own rewards and punishments than with the growth of their subordinates. In fact, they are fearful of having subordinates who are too competent – they worry about having their own weaknesses shown up."*[7]

I then came across this passage in Maslow where he talks about the needs that motivate human behaviour and makes the point that all human behaviour is not necessarily moti-

---

5   There is no recognition of the other needs of people who do to work each day.

6   Prof D McGregor, *The Human Side of Enterprise*, 25th edn, McGraw Hill, 1985, pp 148.

7   ibid., p. 199.

vated by conventional needs such as hunger or the desire for wealth. He then goes on

> *"Most neurotic symptoms or trends amount*
> *to basic need-gratification-bent impulses that*
> *have somehow got stymied or misdirected or*
> *confused with other needs or fixated on the*
> *wrong means. Other symptoms, however, are no*
> *longer gratification-bent but are simply protective*
> *or defensive. They have no goal but to prevent*
> *further hurt or frustration. The difference is like*
> *that between the fighter who still hopes to win*
> *and the one who has no hope of winning, trying*
> *only to lose as painlessly as possible."*[8]

This is a bit of a mouthful; however, if I am right after many years of observation, it is a fact that a huge percentage of the population suffer from a sense of insecurity with diminished self-esteem. Many people become accepting of what they believe to be their own inadequacy whereas others cannot bring themselves to accept this and seek out situations of authority where they can be seen to be confident and authoritative by actually giving orders in circumstances where they give the impression that they know what they are doing. Many such people end up in senior positions of management with frightful consequences because, to the extent that their subordinates might have great potential, they are prevented from bringing that potential to bear on the issues confronting the enterprise and end up being mechanistic pawns doing the bidding of a self-doubting tyrant who can never admit his or her faults. The Theory X

---

8   AH Maslow, *Motivation and Personality*, 2nd edn, Harper & Row, 1970, p. 30.

organization described by McGregor with which we dealt in Chapter 6 abounds with such catastrophes and it is amazing how industry achieves the extraordinary results when such potential is never brought to bear on the undertakings of the enterprise of industry.

People engaged in organizations that fall into the category of Theory X might personally possess good memories but they might not necessarily have good memories of their experiences in the work place.

DEBT

At times a business might find it necessary to borrow and it might also find the process difficult. When a decision is made to borrow money it is important to go through a checklist. The first is to determine how the loan is to be repaid because that is the nature of borrowing and lending. It is always easier to borrow money than it is to repay. Borrowing, no matter how difficult the process; is the easy part. It is the repayment part that is difficult. This lesson was learnt well into the business career of no less a person than Rupert Murdoch.

In an extensive article in the *Australian Financial Times*[1] the author explains in great detail the near catastrophe that visited News Corporation, which had borrowed extensively in its dramatic expansion into one of the world's leading media players. The company had run up $US 2.9 billion of debt owing to one hundred and forty six banks in varying amounts, with many of the loans maturing at different times. Some of the loans were short term, borrowed on the assumption that their renewal or replacement would be a

---

1   *Australian Financial Times,* April 16 1991.

matter of course. In other words, repayment was going to be arranged by a renewal of the loan or by persuading other banks to take over the facility. In 1990, there was what we used to call a credit crisis (this was until we discovered what a real credit crisis was in 2008/09) and banks not only were refusing to renew loans that were falling due but it became almost impossible to gain fresh credit. The refusal of a small bank to play the game of restructuring almost brought News Corporation to collapse, only to be saved by a savvy woman adviser. Taking out a loan without knowing how it is going to be repaid invites financial disaster. A knock on the door by a bank can start a series of crisis from fire sales of valuable assets to bankruptcy.

All businesses should have a philosophy about debt so that before making a decision to borrow, there are clear guidelines that indicate the reason for borrowing and how the loans will be repaid. Borrowing has to be associated with strategy. Too frequently, businesses borrow because "we have a cash flow problem" without looking at why that cash flow problem exists or how it is to be rectified. Sadly, businesses that perhaps have a salvage value or can be turned around with a different strategy; move to the borrowing phase without such a strategy. In those cases, the balance sheet might still look attractive enough to a bank to lend on the security of the balance sheet, but if there is no strategy for repayment of the debt other than a hope and a prayer, the result will be a depreciation of the equity in the business.

There are several reasons for borrowing.

The first is to enable the acquisition of an asset. That asset may be a piece of equipment or another business. This is where some terrible mistakes are made. Often when one company decides to acquire another, they do sums and determine that the increased cash flow from the acquisition will service the debt. Such assumptions have often proved heroic. It is amazing how often due diligence has failed to identify some of the fundamental and underlying problems of the company to be acquired. This is where it is critical to have some idea of the "informal organization"[2]. WorldCom was a corporation that emerged as one of the big players in the US telecommunications industry in the nineties of the last century. It attained its size and status by a series of acquisitions funded by borrowings that were intended to be serviced by the leveraging of the performance of the acquired companies. In the end, to stay afloat, the company fraudulently manipulated its accounts to sustain its share price and meet borrowing covenants. The fraud was discovered by virtue of secret investigations. When the fraud was brought to the attention of the board, the company went into bankruptcy and its CEO was sent to prison for twenty five years.

Whether it is borrowing money to buy equipment, a motor vehicle or another company, there is a basic principle of debt that is avoided at great peril. When taking on debt it has to be clear that the debt can be serviced from existing cash flow. That is a real stopper because often it is thought that the acquisition will increase the cash flow and therefore enable the servicing of the debt.

I am reminded of a sad story from my earlier life as a lawyer. I was approached by a farmer who had the idea of leasing his neighbour's farm for a year. He intended to

2   See *The Theory of the Organization* Chapter 6.

borrow money from the bank to service the lease on the basis that the yield from the farm would be much more than the debt. It was one of these great quick "in and out" deals. He showed me his calculations and they indicated an impressive profit. I had a couple of difficulties with the proposition. The first was that this guy was relying on the cash flow from the acquired asset to fund the loan and in principle, I didn't like that. The other was that crops are incredibly dependent upon the season. A bad season and you can be wiped out, while a good season can be quite profitable. I asked this guy whether he had any divine knowledge of how the season would pan out and he said he didn't but things had been pretty good. I advised him against the deal. Twelve months later, to his credit, the guy came to see me and told me that he wished he had taken my advice because the season failed and he was still lumbered with the debt.

In taking on debt for the purpose of an acquisition, even when it can be demonstrated that the loan can be serviced from existing cash flow, it is also necessary to determine what value the acquisition will create for the customer that will translate into additional revenue. This is the strategic aspect of borrowing.

The process is simple. "Can I afford to service this debt from the existing cash flow of my business?" If the answer is "No" and you are dependent upon the acquired asset to service the debt then you are entering into the sphere of speculation. Sometimes speculative ventures pay off handsomely and other times they are disaster. The test then becomes "if this doesn't work, will it cause me serious financial damage?" Here you are entering into the area of risk management. If the answer is that the damage of failure will be unbearable financial pain; then don't go ahead with taking on the debt.

The next question is "will this debt bring benefits to my customers" and if the answer is "I am not sure" you are running the risk of alienating your customers and thereby eroding the basis for debt servicing.

I am sure that if the Executives of AOL and Time Warner had asked these questions and obtained disinterested and honest answers, the catastrophic merger would never have occurred[3].

I believe that on one occasion, The Greyhound Bus Line Company embarked upon an electronic ticketing service. Customers were used to going to the depot and simply picking up a ticket and getting on the bus. The new ticketing innovation, which cost Greyhound a substantial amount of money it didn't have, resulted in customer defection rather than customer accumulation.

If we successfully negotiate all of these obstacles, the next big issue is, "will I have to pass on the cost or part of the cost of this acquisition to the customer?" What we are talking about here is a price increase. Warning bells are ringing. However, if it can be established that the borrowings will not only result in the maintenance or enhancement of existing customer benefits along with the maintenance of price at existing levels or even with a price reduction, you are in the clear.

Unfortunately, debt is so often taken on in the hopes that the good times will come again. There is that old saying,

---

3   This and other failed mergers and acquisitions are discussed in an article in the *Harvard Business Review*. D Harding & S Rovit, 'Building deals on bedrock', *Harvard Business Review,* September 2004, p. 121.

"When you are in a hole, stop digging". It is much better to cut one's losses when they are small than when they are large.

If a business is in a hole then it is time to stop digging and to find a strategy or, if you like, a step ladder to get out of the hole. Debt may be part of that strategy but it has to be accompanied by a strategy that will get you onto a profitable road where it is possible to service the debt. Sometimes, there are solutions to pressing financial problems that do not involve debt. In fact, when I go into a distressed company, it is unlikely in the extreme that the bank will come along offering a loan.

I remember on one occasion I was called into an engineering company that had a negative cash flow and things were quite bad. They were in the middle of a serious recession that was the aftermath of that period in a business cycle when everyone believes the good times will never come to an end. The work for this business had seriously contracted but nevertheless, it did have work coming in and ongoing projects. Paying its bills was the problem and one bill in particular was the rent of several floors of a City building at pre-recession rental prices. Part of the premises was occupied by a business that had been "acquired". There was value in the business to the people running it, but none for my client so we negotiated a sale of that business (which ultimately folded) and this reduced the rent. We then re-examined the need for space and with a little bit of thought it became clear that we could accommodate everyone on one floor. So we went to the landlord and said that we wanted to be there for the long haul, and could we negotiate a reduction in rent and a rental holiday? The landlord realised that having a tenant paying some rent was better than no tenant paying any rent and agreed to rewrite the lease.

Suddenly, there was cash in the bank and a positive cash flow (there were some other tricks that brought this about). The firm was behind the eight ball so far as technology was concerned and it had been considering expensive financing for new technology which was not only necessary from a competitive point of view but from the point of view of being able to service customers effectively. We didn't want a huge debt-servicing load to suddenly impact on the beautiful financial scenario we had just engineered so we went to the bank with a positive cash flow and asked them for an interest only loan for two years to reequip the place with the latest technology. After demonstrating the ability to service the debt from existing cash flow, the bank agreed. The business has never looked back and is now a leader in its industry.

Another alternative to debt is capital raising. This is a tricky area and one where there are a lot of grey zones that enable people to sometimes claim they are injecting capital into their business and on other occasions claim that they are lending money to the business. This trail becomes even more complicated when people don't understand the difference between debt and capital.

Let us start with the example used in the section on accounting and let us suppose that the football star actually had $1,000 in his bank. He uses this to commence his business and opens a bank account for the business and pays the $1,000 into that account. Suddenly, there are two entities in existence. One is the personal entity of the footballer and the other is the business entity. So far as business, accounting and the law are concerned, they are two distinct entities and each has to deal with one another at arm's length. The footballer has to make a choice at the time of the payment of the $1,000 to his business. Will the $1,000 be a loan to the business or will it be capital? The difference is profound. If the $1,000 is treated as a loan it means that the business owes the footballer $1,000 and is beholden to him. If it is capital, it means that his $1,000 is converted into shares in the company and the company owes him nothing. However, if the company grows and its balance sheet constantly discloses that the assets are increasing, then the value of the shares increase and the $1,000 becomes worth more. The value of the company might have doubled, thus making the shares worth twice as much as they were initially.

If, on the other hand, the footballer makes a loan to the company and it repays him, the footballer still has his $1000 plus his company which is hopefully increasing in value. Suppose he started the company with a loan of $1,000 but with one issued share of $1. The capital of the company would be $1 and it would owe the footballer $1,000. However, after the repayment of the loan to the footballer it is likely that, at a minimum, the $1 share will be worth $1,000 and the company will have no debt. In other words, the share will have increased in value by 1000%.

In a simple way, this discloses the beauty of debt to capital. However, enormous care has to be exercised when making a decision about funding a company.

Capital is necessary to start a company. Once the company gets going and it decides that it requires further funds for expansion it then has the choice of going to the shareholders and asking them to buy more shares in the company or going to the bank and borrowing the money. The rules for a company borrowing money are just the same as those I have explained earlier in this essay.

In the financial crisis a lot of banks went to the market and issued new shares at prices less than the prices quoted on the stock exchange. Why did they do that? The initial answer is that capital is not debt and by issuing capital rather than borrowing money, the balance sheet is increased in dollar terms by the amount of capital raised and that capital does not have to be repaid. Suddenly the banks had billions more in money which offset to a certain extent their borrowings. They shored up their balance sheet.

There were more fundamental reasons that the banks didn't borrow money. The first was that they couldn't as no one would lend to them other than the poor suckers in the street who deposited any spare cash they had with the banks and became exposed to the risk of the bank collapsing. The second reason is that it would have worsened rather than improved their balance sheet. Accordingly, this decision of companies to raise money by issuing capital to shareholders is an indication that it can't borrow the money. That is not always the case, but generally a capital raising is the second best option for achieving an inflow of money into a company.

The explanation is simple and is exactly the same as the example of the footballer business. The footballer was smart and decided to just lend the $1,000 to the company because he realised that if the company came good, he would have his $1,000 back and still own the company. The shares would then be worth more than the $1 he contributed initially. Suppose a company has 1000 shares on issue and borrows $1,000 to develop the business, either by way of acquisition or organic growth, and gradually pays off the debt but increases the value of the company to say $2,000. The company is debt free and still only has 1,000 shares on issue. In this case, the 1000 shares become worth $2,000, thus doubling the shareholder value. However, if, instead of borrowing the $1,000 the company issued 1000 additional shares then the value of the company would have to be divided amongst 2000 shares rather than 1,000. In this case, even if the value of the company doubled, the share value would not have increased. That is why the market frowns on companies issuing shares to grow rather than borrowing money. The market says that share issues "dilute" the capital, resulting in more shares participating in the profits and assets of the firm. The market also frowns on borrowings unless they see that the company can conform with the rules just outlined in the earlier segment of this piece. In fact, often when a company resorts to a capital raising it puts the wind up investors. Once the banks restored their balance sheets after the financial crisis, a number of them went to the market to borrow and the offerings were oversubscribed because there were a lot of very cheap assets available for banks at distressed prices and the market was happy to lend money to the banks to accumulate these cheap assets.

That does not say that borrowing is a fantastic strategy unless it can be justified according to the various criteria discussed. The rules can be summarised:

1. Is there a degree of certainty that the debt can be serviced from existing cash flow?
2. Is the borrowing accompanied by a sound strategy for improving the financial performance of the business?

3. If something goes wrong and the business can't service the debt from existing cash flow, what are the consequences and can they be tolerated?
4. Will the money enable the business to generate additional benefits to the customer that will result in additional profits and assets for the business;
5. Will the business be passing on the cost of the borrowings to the customer without an equal or greater benefit?
6. Will all of this result in increasing the value to the shareholder?

You will note that only after going through the first five steps do we come to that critical issue of shareholder value. Current mantra is that the reason for the existence of the corporation is to enhance shareholder value. I believe that is a consequence and not a reason. Shareholder value is directly related to the ability of a company to deliver benefits to customers that equal or exceed the expectations of the customer for a price that delivers a profit to the company. By achieving that profit, the value of the company increases, as does the value of the shares held by the shareholder. Shares are worthless unless the company can deliver this social benefit.

Debt has its function and is critical to the smooth operation of commercial society. On the other hand it can generate a process which ends up in bankruptcy and I suspect that in most cases of company failure, the inability to service debt is the triggering mechanism. I might add that the debt issue will be a triggering mechanism and not the fundamental cause of business failure. More often than not, the failure will be the inability of the business to provide benefits to customers that equal or exceed their expectations at a price that guarantees the financial success of the business.

DEBTORS

This is the second of the three D's and just as important in the context of the financial health of the corporation.

As we have learnt, "debtors" is that category of financial functions that represent the money owed to the corporation. It is brought to account in the balance sheet as an asset. Oh my goodness! Therein lies the slippery slope that many have taken to bankruptcy. Debtors are people who owe money to the company. In other words, they are supposed to have in their pockets the cash that should be in the bank account of the company.

Businesses that extend credit generally specify trading terms. For instance, a typical trading term for a business is "cash thirty days"[1]. Very often I go into a business and discover that some debtors go way out beyond thirty days and sometimes into many months. On too many occasions I have seen debtors go out beyond twelve months. I talk

---

[1] I would have to say that my trading terms are cash on receipt of invoice. The reason is that when I complete a project I sit down with my clients to determine whether or not they have received value for money. Until then, they have my credit. Once they have agreed that they have value for money, they no longer have credit and I expect cash.

to the finance people and they tell me that so and so is a good customer and will pay eventually. Customers who don't pay are not good customers. Just think about it for a moment. Even customers who are within their trading terms of thirty days have to be funded and there are both direct and indirect costs of funding.

Let me tell you a story about a law firm that operated on time costing. Time was meticulously recorded on each client matter and in fact, the management emphasis of the firm was on achieving a certain monthly amount of time recorded and billed. At the end of the month, the bills went out irrespective of the state of the case. The profit of the firm according to its financial statements was fantastic and its balance sheet was in great shape. The only trouble was that it was having this confounded "cash flow" problem. In order to address it, the firm went to the bank for ever-increasing facilities based on its financial statements and on the basis that the debtors were considered "assets". By the time I came in, the bank's patience was at an end and decided not to extend the facility any longer. Without collecting the debts, the firm could fold. Regrettably, when we looked at many of the debts, they were in relation to the cost of time spent on a client matter rather than results achieved. The area of law in which the firm practised was such that many of the customers were unable to pay their bills until their matter was complete. By concentrating on the one overarching KPI of the firm, which was to get bills out at the end of each month, people lost site of the necessity to actually bring matters to early finality, thus compounding their problems. Most of the debts in this case were not capable of being collected given the current state of the client's legal affairs.

By the time we had reconstructed the balance sheet on the basis of discounting much of the debtors, things looked sick. Fortunately we had a few other options to turn the ship around.

A construction company does a lot of work before it is paid but generally has an administrator on site to keep a check on what has been done in the month and then prepares an invoice which is discussed with the customer or project manager. Payment is generally made within days of the invoice, otherwise a good construction company will stop work. However, there is a part of the calculation of the value of work done that is not invoiced and it is called a "retention" allowance. This is an mount retained by the customer as an insurance against completion. The retention allowance is not paid until all aspects of the project are completed to the satisfaction of the customer. This allowance is generally 5% of the total cost of the project.

The balance sheet of this company was fantastic. No debt, some cash in the bank and a healthy net assets balance. The only trouble I had was that in talking to a lot of people working in the business they indicated that the company had a reputation for not completing projects and that it was the devil's own trouble to get it back and finish jobs to meet customer complaints. When I matched this information up with the balance sheet and financial statements, I noticed that the invoiced revenue for the firm was $X million. I concluded that if the firm was in fact completing projects to the satisfaction of customers that retention amount should roughly equal 5% of the annual revenue. In fact the retention amount shown as an "asset" in the balance sheet equalled

20% of the annual revenue. Anyone in the construction industry will tell you that a lot of this is unrecoverable as the company has decided that it would cost more to rectify than to write off the amount. Millions of dollars were unrecoverable! Rather than an asset, most of the retention amount was a liability and had to be written off.

Just by way of interest, I then looked at the creditors (the businesses to which the company owed money) and found that there were debts going out beyond ninety days and some of them into one hundred and twenty days. I did a quick sum to see what would happen if all of the creditors insisted upon paying within the trading terms and this indicated that the bank would be overdrawn by a massive amount. Rather than borrowing money from the bank and paying fees and interest, this company had been able to persuade its suppliers to fund the company at no interest.

By the time the balance sheet was reconstructed and ample provision made for the debtors that were never going to be collected, the company had net liabilities.

In my first lesson in academia about turnarounds Professor John Whitney at Colombia talked about one of his experiences and indicated that the first thing you do when you look at the debtors of a company is talk to the long-term debtors. He indicated (and I have born this out time and again) that quite often people don't pay because they feel that they have not had value for their money (remember the theory of exchange[2]?). You don't go asking them for money but you try to find out what is wrong with the company. Where you go to collect money is from the people who are within the trading terms. Accordingly, one

2   See Chapter 3.

has to be careful about treating debtors as an asset because so very frequently it will be discovered that once they are outside the trading terms, the difficulty in collecting those debts increases dramatically.

The best way to avoid having debtors is not to extend credit. There is sufficient credit extended in a business by virtue of the stock or infrastructure that a business has to carry in order to deliver benefits to the customer. Once those benefits are delivered then credit should run out. Often, credit is extended to enable a sale which means that without credit a sale would not occur. In that case, a business should examine the quality of its offering.

A recurrent phenomenon experienced by smaller firms is the occasion on which they believe they have snared a major corporation as a customer. I remember one industrial supplier which had taken on a well-established public company (and its balance sheet was in great shape). On investigation it appeared that to snare this customer the margins were as thin as a razor blade. Once you have margins that thin, you need to get cash otherwise the cost of funding a customer results in loss. However, this particular customer, in addition to getting finer margins than any of the other customers of this supplier, wasn't paying. It was the worst payer on the books. When asked to bring their account within trading terms their reply was "if you want our business we set the terms". To its credit, the small business let that customer pay its bills and then set its terms with another supplier. The small business survived and is doing well.

If a company decides to be in the business of providing credit, it is getting out of its core business because that is the business of banks and history indicates that they are not very good at their core business. However, if credit is one of the aspects of selling it is critical that debtors be not allowed to get beyond the trading terms. Too often, people don't start chasing debtors until they are well outside the trading terms whereas the moment someone gets outside the trading terms danger bells are ringing and that is the time to act.

One common response I have had when inquiring from people why they have not paid, the reply is "so and so said it wasn't necessary until I had on-sold it to a customer". The "so and so" was a sales person on commission who has disappeared from the scene with her or his commission. If you get onto it early enough, you can chase up with the errant sales person to check to see whether in fact he or she did indicate trading terms beyond the trading policy of the company. Frequently, you get an ambiguous response "Well, not in so many words" which of course, translated to English means "Precisely".

Debtors are not an asset until paid and when relying on them as an asset in the balance sheet, extreme care should be exercised.

DEPRECIATION

I want to devote this section to one simple aspect of accounting called "depreciation". The extent to which it is misunderstood in management, particularly in smaller organizations, is monumental and causes enormous difficulties, the reason being similar to the reason that management sometimes confuses profits as disclosed in an accrual based profit and loss account with cash in the bank.

I am sure everyone knows how depreciation works and so forgive me for going over this stuff again. However the number of people who tell me that they understand how depreciation works and still get into difficulties by ignoring its basic principles is legendary.

A business purchases some equipment. In order to make the example understandable across industries, let us say the business purchases $100,000 of computers. This $100,000 is a big hit in the business as its gross income is $200,000 and its net profit is $50,000. If it wrote off the entire cost of the equipment in the year of purchase it would result in a loss of $50,000. The CEO mightn't like that but there is another interested party which would like it less and that is the silent partner called the "Taxation Department" or "The Inland Revenue Authority". You simply don't have to pay tax on losses. This is where the concept of depreciation comes into play.

When a business acquires what we call a "depreciable asset" such as machinery or a computer installation, it involves expenditure which doesn't fall into the ordinary category of expenditure because it is generally non-recurring. For instance, if a business acquires a major computer installation, it looks forward to getting many years of use out of that investment. Accordingly, revenue authorities require that the cost of that installation be written off over a period of years rather than being a deduction against income in the year the computers were acquired. In the example in the previous paragraph, $100,000 goes out the door. The business can't claim that as a deduction against profit in the year the money is spent. It is required to write the amount off over a period of years. This process of writing it off over a period of years is called "depreciation"

There are accounting and regulatory rules about depreciation which indicate the method of calculation. Let us take the more simple method which is the fixed rate method in which the equipment is written off (depreciated) to nothing over five years by allowing a depreciation rate of 20%.

If we use the example of $100,000 spent on computers, in the first year of purchase, the equipment is depreciated by 20% which means that an amount of $20,000 is allowed as a deduction against revenue. It is just like paying salaries of $20,000 so far as the preparation of the profit and loss account is concerned except that in this case, the money may already have been paid. Each year, the business is allowed a deduction of $20,000 until the equipment is completely written off.

While this is good for the revenue authorities in one sense, it is also good for the business in a completely different sense because it is intended to introduce a discipline into the financial management of a business that will protect the business from having to put up with outmoded or worn out equipment.

Let us suppose that the business paid cash for the equipment. It is down $100,000 in the bank account. Now this is where management and particularly owner management make some silly mistakes. The $100,000 has gone out the door and replaced by computers that probably aren't worth much after a year. Each year, the business reduces its income for taxation purposes by $20,000 and management forgets that at the end of the five year period, there won't be any more deductions and it will be necessary to replace that equipment. What should happen is that the $20,000 that has been deducted as a depreciation expense should be set aside in a special depreciation account so that at the end of five years, when the time comes to replace the equipment, there will be money in the bank to do so. Do you know how rarely this happens? Management will often be provided with a financial statement called "Source and application of funds" and because the amount of depreciation has not actually gone out in cash, management will receive an indication in relation to depreciation of a positive cash flow of $20,000. There is a tendency to forget that this is related to depreciation with the result that it is looked upon as surplus cash and spent on items or people who do not bring value to the customer. When the time comes to replace the equipment, and there is no cash in the tin management says "Oh, we will just make it last another year". That makes the staff upset and hurts the customer which expects to be serviced by the most up to date technology. It diminishes the competitive position of the business.

If the twenty thousand was in fact placed in a depreciation account, it would mean that at the end of the five-year period, the $100,000 plus interest would be there waiting for reinvestment. Because the price of technology decreases each year, the $100,000 plus interest would buy a lot more technology than it bought five years ago and the business can then take a technological competitive advantage.

That is not the end of depreciation by any means. You might recall the discussion on the balance sheet of the company[1]. The Balance Sheet as you will recall is where the assets and liabilities of the company are recorded. Sometimes the balance sheet is also used by management to demonstrate the financial health of the business. Once equipment is purchased, it shows up in the balance sheet as an asset. There is a tendency to take the asset into the balance sheet at cost. So, in the case of the $100,000 of computer equipment that we just mentioned, once the transaction went through and assuming cash was paid out of the funds of the business the balance sheet would show the asset of $100,000. However the bank balance would reduce by $100,000. In this transaction, the net assets or liabilities of the business would remain the same. In the following year, the computer asset would be shown as $80,000 (after depreciation of 20%). However, we all know that this will not be a true reflection of the value of the asset. Suppose you tried to sell

---

1   See Chapter 5.

the used computer equipment! What would you get for it if you could find a buyer? It is superseded equipment and the current equivalent will have more capacity and bells and whistles and will be cheaper. The true value of the equipment will be a lot less than $80,000 with the result that the balance sheet will not be providing an accurate statement of the affairs of the business. The equipment only has salvage value. This is how the balance sheet can play tricks. Accordingly whenever management is looking at the balance sheet it is necessary to remember that any equipment on the books only has salvage value and that may be a lot less than the value accredited to it in the balance sheet. That is why it is so necessary to make cash provision for the amount of depreciation written off each year.

The problem gets a little more complicated. With big expenditure items, businesses often resort to some form of financing. The business might borrow the money outright and use it to pay cash to the vendor or it might enter into some purchase agreement by way of hire purchase or lease. These transactions keep management honest, because what goes out of the account in these cases is cash. In this case the source and application of funds will be a more accurate statement of the cash position of the business. However, when the financial agreement comes to an end, there will still be the necessity to fund the acquisition of new equipment. This is another trap because management sees that it can get a cash break by keeping the equipment going when the lease or mortgage payments[2] expire. Here is a great opportunity to improve the cash position of the business by running the old equipment when it is no longer attracting monthly expenditure.

That is fine to a point, but if in fact the equipment is out of date and your competitors have more up to date equipment and steal a competitive advantage, then it might be a case of penny wise and dollar foolish.

I have seen management really play around with this deprecation issue and make accounting arrangements that do not reflect the true nature of the financial arrangements so as to indicate a better cash position than is in fact the case. As is so often said, "there is no such thing as a free lunch", with the result that innovative or aggressive accounting, no matter how legal it might be (and generally it isn't), has a day of reckoning. All of the financial scandals that we hear about have their origins in a few small tricks at the beginning to make the books look better than the actual financial state of affairs of the company. It could even be as simple as playing around with depreciation. Once management starts this journey, they often find it difficult to recover, with the result that the accounting tricks become more and more aggressive and more and more damaging to the sustainability of the business. Just ask the guys at Enron (those who aren't in prison or dead).

---

2   With lease payments it is a bit trickier because the business doesn't actually own the equipment. Many lease agreements have a provision that the business can acquire the equipment for a final cash payment which is often minimal depending on the terms of the lease. However, some people go into a lease for lower monthly repayments and a high repayment at the end. When the end comes, they sometimes don't have the cash and have to go cap in hand again to the finance company to extend the lease, thus resulting in using old equipment and eroding the competitive advantage of the business

CHANGE

Plus ca change, plus c'est la même chose is a phrase that was coined by a Jean-Baptiste Alphonse Karr in 1849 and has become an accepted description of organizations and governments that pretend to change but in fact revert to the status quo. I think its translated meaning is "The more things change the more they stay the same".

I shudder whenever I hear people talking about bringing in a "Change expert". I have never met a person who considers themselves to be a change expert, but I have met a few CEOs who believe that their role is to bring about change and they set to with a passion to change things without quite understanding what it is that they are changing.

I want to go back to the section in which we talked about the Hawthorne experiments and discussed the various contributions to management literature by Chester Barnard, Peter Drucker and Professor Douglas McGregor. You will recall that one of the phenomena that these guys identified in businesses was the emergence within businesses of what has become known as "informal organizations". These informal organizations tend to form when there is an absence of effective communication with management to the point that management objectives are either not understood by those with the responsibility for their implementation or they are considered to be inappropriate or likely to be ineffective. A certain distrust of management emerges and people start doing things their own way.

There was the classic story of the people in the bank wiring room in the Hawthorne experiments who between themselves had an understanding that they would limit output for fear that if they increased their output, management might change the rules of their engagement and remuneration. Management was unaware of this situation and that is why we call it an "informal organization". They are to be found throughout the business community as well as within government and not for profit organizations and it is quite challenging to think of the impact that this phenomenon has on the effectiveness of organizations. Quite frequently the effect is negative and in an instinctive way, management knows that there is something not quite right with the result that the role of the new CEO is to "change" the culture of the organization.

The frustration that is often expressed by CEOs as to how difficult it is to change the culture is explicable by virtue of the fact that there is little recognition on their part as to what is the culture of the organization. They only see the manifestation of the informal organization but are unaware of its existence. Without this awareness, coupled with a lack of understanding of the reason for its existence, the task of change is hopeless and at the end of the day, things just remain the same.

What a lot of people don't realise is that all organizations have a culture and as we have pointed out earlier, that culture is the aggregation of the knowledge, wisdom, experience, emotions and personalities of the people who work in the organization.

It is one thing to alter the direction of the organization or change its strategy or business plan, but another to alter the culture of the organization because it exists either informally or formally within the aggregate of the people.

I am reminded of a story. In my previous life as a lawyer, I had a client who had been defrauded of a large amount of money in a money market transaction and the person who had defrauded him disappeared. I was given the task of getting the money back! For some reason or another that I can't remember, I had a suspicion that this guy was in Los Angeles. I spoke with the Los Angeles Police Department who said that they thought that American Express might have some knowledge about the guy. I then met with one of the AMEX credit card fraud investigators who had been a member of the LAPD. He told me about his job and the fact that research consistently discloses that of all people involved in the use of credit cards, only three per cent were dishonest.

I always remember that when I go into an organization and feel that it is safe to assume that almost all if not all the people in the organization are honest. In a beautiful, if rather technical book, a leading Japanese authority on Total Quality Management and Total Quality Control discussed this issue of people in the enterprise of business, particularly in relation to the extensive practice of supervision and inspection in Western Industries. He was making the point that if you can manufacture something without defects, then you don't need supervision or inspection. However, he went further because of a tendency not to trust employees to do their best. He made the point that most people are good and want to do their best (echoes of AMEX credit card experience)[1].

Can I add my own experience from the many interviews I have conducted in the work place? Consistently, in interviews, employees tell me of their frustrations and these relate to the inability of the business to achieve optimal outcomes. They are at the coal face and they know how the business is going and how its competitors are going and if the business is not doing as well as it should, people get very upset. This is not what management expects to discover when these interviews take place. Management expects the staff to complain that they aren't getting paid enough and will whinge about things that concern them personally. People are basically good and want to do their best and they get frustrated if they are prevented from doing so. Therein lies the culture of the organization. It is already there wanting to be harnessed. It is like a fractious horse at the barrier wanting to get going, only to find that it is restrained. It is that culture of people earnestly wanting to do their best that exists in almost all businesses[2]and when a CEO comes in, all that he or she has to do is harness that energy and the business will take off.

I cannot recall going into an organization with any pre-

---

1 K Ishikawa, *What is total quality control? The Japanese Way*, Prentice Hall, 1985.

2 I am fearful that these days, commercial banks and financial institutions are employing people that are too focused on making money with the result that in an ethical sense, they might not be as committed to doing their "best" in an ethical sense as a lot of people on the factory floor.

fixed concept of what I was going to do. All I have ever done is feed off this wisdom of the masses of people in the organization who generally know what is wrong and what needs to be done, but can't do anything about it. If you can gain their trust, short of some catastrophic financial scenario, nothing will stop the organization from prospering.

What I like to do when I go into an organization is harness the culture while changing direction.

As we have learnt from Maslow, people have aspirations. I don't care who they are, they have dreams of being something special, even if it just means winning the school raffle. Everyone loves to be recognised for doing something well and worthwhile. Everyone yearns for their place in the sun. They don't want to be celebrities in the sense of most of the flawed characters that parade as such, but everyone does seek and yearn for recognition. If a person comes up with an idea in the work place and the boss says "that's not a bad idea we will give it a go and see what happens" that person goes home that evening in a state of joy and wants to share the experience with a husband, wife, mother, father, boyfriend, kids or whoever. "Guess what happened at work today? The boss thought my idea was great". There are so many of those ideas in the work place, and if management wants to tap into the culture of that huge source of potential, they have to engage with the people and give them recognition.

One Friday evening and it was past five which was the closing time for one of the clinics of a huge radiology business that I was evaluating prior to taking on the role of CEO. Everyone had gone home and I was running late and there was one more person to interview. I told her that I could come back next week, but she insisted that we go ahead even though she wasn't getting paid for staying overtime. She was an administrative person who acted as a receptionist and typist. About two hours later I knew all about that business and what was wrong and what needed to be done to fix it. This person was so desperate for the business to do well but so frustrated that she had no influence in the organization.

The owners of the business were shocked when I appointed her HR Manager but she had the support of all the staff and did a fantastic job. She was particularly concerned when issues came up that required expenditure and she became a sort of gatekeeper. She was perhaps more driven than a lot of people, but she represents the type of energy that can make the culture of an organization. This energy and passion is possessed to a greater or lesser degree by all but 3% of the population and more than likely, that 3% segment is not represented to that extent in most workplaces.

That woman went on to do her MBA and ended up in some big job in a different organization.

When I hear people say they are going to change the organization, that's fine. But when I hear them say they are going to change the culture I hesitate. Sure, there is sometimes a culture in organizations such as Enron and in some banks where money drives people and the culture is disgraceful[3], but you can't tell me that underneath it all, there are many people in the organization who are offended at what is going on and want to do something about it. When a bunch of crooks get hold of the steering

---

3   A description of the culture in the trading room at Enron can be found in B Cruver, *Enron: The Anatomy of Greed,* Arrow Press, 2003, pp. 30-33, 209-210.

wheel or a CEO who wants to make a quick buck with the share options that have been issued, terrible things happen in a business[4]. However, my experience is that many good people leave that organization; that informal organizations emerge that resist the direction of the business and most find the direction personally objectionable. That is when the CEO loses the "culture" of the organization and it is heading for trouble.

If a business isn't doing well and there is a need to change direction, then nothing is going to work unless the direction has the enthusiastic support of those good people in the organization who want to do their best. Don't insult them by telling them that they have to change who they are because who they are is the strength of the organization. Don't insult them by implying that they are dishonest, because only 3% of the population are truly dishonest. Don't tell them that you know best, without first discovering what they know and think, because the likelihood is that they know and think quite a lot which could be good for the business. Don't tell them that you are going to motivate them, because you can't. The only way people can be motivated is by having in place systems that enable them to achieve their potential.

One of the sadder aspects of management literature is the speed with which seminal material is forgotten. I have mentioned earlier in this book some of those texts, but I now want to introduce another. In a sense it is perhaps the most significant book on management ever written, however, it

---

4   See BJ Hall, R Khurana & C Madigan, 'Al Dunlap at Sunbeam', *Harvard Business Review*, April 12 1999.

is associated with the quality movement and of course, we have moved on since then. The book is *Out of the Crisis*[5] by Edwards Deming, one of the founders of the Japanese quality movement. Deming was a statistician, not a writer, with the result that the book has little literary merit and requires a modicum of statistical knowledge. One of the issues that concerned Deming was the immediate reaction of management to seek out someone to blame when something went wrong. Unfortunately, this is still a recurrent phenomenon today, despite Deming.

With convincing statistical arguments he demonstrated that there are two types of mistake. One is what he calls a "special cause" when the mistake can be traced to a specific event such as an error of a worker. The other cause is what he calls a "common cause" where a mistake can be attributed to the system in which people work and is therefore systemic and more likely ends up being the responsibility of management. Statistically, it is established that the majority of mistakes in organizations have a common cause or are a result of a systemic failure.

Deming gives many examples, but one that I always think about when I am giving a presentation or a talk is about a parcel service in Vancouver. Management was very concerned about the performance of one driver because of the fact that he was always very late with his round, causing delays in delivery. Management considered that the driver's performance was poor and not surprisingly, were considering firing him. Deming persuaded them to let him go out with the driver. It turned out that his route was in very hilly parts of Vancouver, with the result that

5   W Edwards Deming, *Out of the Crisis,* 18th edn, CUP, 1992.

when he was in Valleys, his radio transmission didn't work and he found it difficult to make contact with customers. Accordingly, he would go out of his way to some vantage point so that he could make radio contact. His customers thought that he was fantastic and realised the extent to which he went to service them. It did appear that he had consistently complained about the inadequacy of his radio transmission, but management had ignored his complaints because none of the other drivers had any concerns.

This is just another story of the desire of a worker to do his best and only for some sensible intervention; he stood to lose his job and the company a lot of customers.

Deming tells another story of a truck driver who was in trouble because suddenly the consumption of fuel took an alarming leap. Management was considering dealing with the driver until Deming did some statistical analysis and discovered that this thirstiness of the truck had occurred recently. So he sought advice as to the possible causes of increased consumption other than driver misbehaviour. A number of ideas were suggested including spark plugs (before the days of fuel injection). Deming got them to change the spark plugs and consumption returned to normal. He then recommended to management that they have more regular maintenance.

Finally, one other brief story is worthwhile relating. The Motor Equipment Division of the City of Madison had the responsibility of servicing the vehicles of the various departments such as garbage trucks, police cars and city vehicles. There were many complaints to the Mayor about downtime, but management had installed a system of repairs on demand. The mechanics were sick and tired of being blamed for the delays and down time and undertook their own research because they had a pretty good idea of what was wrong. They identified a jeep that cost $4,200 to repair. It was used to haul salt in the winter and had corroded. Early maintenance in a comprehensive maintenance programme would have resulted in the expenditure of $164, which would have prevented corrosion. The mechanics got together and presented the Mayor with a broken piston with a large amount of steel exhaust jammed into it. After the Mayor had accepted this gift, the mechanics then presented the Mayor with a spring that cost $1.50. They indicated that the cost of repairs to the vehicle with the smashed piston was $3,200, but with regular maintenance, sixteen of these springs would have been fitted and that would have avoided the disaster. The Mayor was reported to have said:

> *"You know how to find problems; you know how to fix them and wish to solve them. We should get out of your way and let you do it."*

Day in and day out I come across similar stories where employees know what is wrong with the organization, they know what to do to fix it but have no power to do so. And these are the organizations to which change gurus come along and say "we are going to change the culture here". How indecently insulting!

Since the days of the Hawthorne experiments in the thirties we have known of the enormous potential of people if we just treat them like adults and trust them. If we consult with them in an atmosphere of trust rather than one of suspicion (which is more often the case with performance reviews) we unlock the potential of the organization. We no longer talk about "empowerment" because the people know they are trusted and will do what is necessary in any situation without the fear of being criticised.

If we put to one side directional changes in organizations, which must be subject to constant competitive review, the only change that is indicated in an organization is when people are not trusted and a gap forms between the objectives of management and those of the employees. Even in so far as directional change is concerned, there is enough evidence that if employees who are going to be affected by the change are consulted and have input into change, the input will be invaluable and the employees will more likely embrace the new direction and not wander off and form their informal organization.

There is a risk that up to 3% of people might not want to go along with the idea or even might want to sabotage the enterprise, but then there is 97% of the workforce just waiting to be involved and recognised.

As we have seen from the marketing segments, the inevitable thrust of business today is to secure ever increasing value for the community at ever decreasing cost. This creates a market of abundance and rather than resulting in less employment opportunities, it results in more, because the wheels of the economy are moving more quickly and everyone is going to benefit. Business organizations are the tool for bringing societal benefits in the way of goods and services and I know that organizations that are highly ethical and have their objective of bringing ever-increasing societal benefits to the population are exciting places to work. They are even more exciting if the organization involves every person in sharing their objective.

You can change direction, but give the people the opportunity to create the culture. If you don't then *Plus ca change, plus c'est la même chose.*

Strangely enough we don't have to look for any exotic new formulae to manage in this new environment because there are enduring principles of management that have been long with us, and in some cases, since the cave men. More recent material emerged in the thirties of the last century and it is to these enduring principles, rather than the latest snake oil which form the foundations of enduring and sustainable enterprises.

On lunch break from lecturing to a class of international business students at an International programme conducted on behalf of the University of California, Riverside, one of the students approached me. Her name was Sophie and she was from Brazil. She said that she wanted to tell me a story that related to the lecture I had just completed. I suggested to her that she might want to share the story with the class and she agreed.

During the afternoon, the opportunity arose and so I announced to the class that Sophie had a story to share with us. Sophie then told this story.

"I had completed my degree in Business Administration but couldn't find a job anywhere and so I took a job as a receptionist. When I first started, the place was terrible. No one talked to one another and everyone seemed angry. The boss was awful and continued to criticise people and make life unpleasant for everyone. Even the customers didn't seem to like being in the place. I would go home upset.

One day I had the idea to do something about it and so I brought a jar of candies to work and placed them on my desk. Gradually, fellow workers would come up to my desk and take a candy and we would then have a chat. Other people then brought candy jars to work and after a while, people would walk up to another person's desk and take a candy and have a chat. Customers would take a candy and then start talking to us. The boss hated it and used to criticise me and whenever he did, I would smile at him.

Customers started to bring flowers into the place. The boss was often angry but couldn't to anything about it and just didn't know what to do when I smiled.

After a while I got another job in management and left".

I then said to Sophie "Did you ever go back". She said that she did and so I asked her what she found when she went back. "Everything had gone back to the way it was when I first started".

How sad! Sophie had discovered the true culture of the place and it was obvious that she had the courage to make it blossom. However, once she left and the boss regained control, the culture was suffocated. The more things change, the more they stay the same.

DEMING

I recently took a weekend off from Thunderbird School of Global Management, which is located in Phoenix Arizona and only a couple of hundred kilometres from the Grand Canyon. It had been snowing heavily and access to the Grand Canyon was difficult. I heard that the road was open on the Friday afternoon and headed off. On the way back on the Sunday I had to take a detour through a little town called Williams and stopped in a café for some lunch. The café was on a corner and I realised that I was fascinated by the cars passing through the intersection. There were the usual suspects of SUV's, but just about every second vehicle was Japanese. I couldn't help but ask myself "how did the Americans, with their phenomenal start in the auto industry, ever let this happen?"

When I returned to work I got a book out of the library called *Out of the Crisis* by W. Edwards Deming[1]. I looked in the back of the book to see how often it had been taken out of the library and found that someone had taken it out in 2002. I then realised why the Americans had been beaten

1   W Edwards Deming, *Out of the Crisis,* 18th edn, CUP, 1992.

to the punch by the Japanese in the manufacture of auto-mobiles as well as electronics.

Deming was born in Sioux City, Iowa, USA on the 14 October 1900. This was an auspicious date because it heralded in the famous twentieth Century. America saw the birth of a huge auto industry that penetrated every Western market and many others. Ford became famous for developing mass production techniques and General Motors established itself at the forefront of progressive management[2]. Deming lived his life contemporaneously with the profound emergence of the industrial society, finally resting eternally on the 20 December 1993, just seven years short of the commencement of another century. During that time we saw the rise and fall of the American auto industry, while that of the Japanese continued to take market share in the traditional home of the automobile. Deming had a significant part to play in the emergence of the Japanese industry and was saddened at the failure of America to compete. So saddened that he wrote the book to which reference was made at the beginning of this chapter, *Out of the Crisis*. He wrote this in 1982, but despite his efforts was unable to gain sufficient voice in his own country until late in his life. At the age of 82, he was engaged for a short time by the Ford Motor Company.

Deming had a background in electrical engineering and statistics. He obtained a PhD from Yale in 1928 and worked in the Bell Telephone Laboratories where he came across another brilliant but little known pioneer in qualify management by the name of Walter Shewart who had invented

---

2   However, Drucker in his book *The Theory of the Corporation* had some reservations about the extent of its progressiveness.

what has come to be known as the "control chart". Shewart was born in 1891 and died in 1967, but introduced Deming to his ideas about statistical control.

After the war, the Japanese decided that it needed to become an industrial power if it was to return a standard of living to the Japanese that had been denied them as a result of the horrific experience of wars with firstly China and then the Western World. Another American pioneer in statistical control, Joseph Juran, had discovered the works of an Italian economist, Vilfredo Pareto[3], and in particular, a statistical tool which was adopted by the Japanese to eliminate variation in product quality. Juran also had a profound influence on the resurgence of Japanese industry but worked independently of Deming. As a result of all this, Deming was invited to Japan to assist Japanese industry development by using his ideas on statistical quality control for which the Japanese became famous. While the American auto industry was recalling cars because of faulty manufacture, the Japanese were building quality into their vehicles that reduced dramatically the need for recall once the product got to the market. Gradually, Japanese quality dominated, not only in the auto industry but also in the electronic industry and then the watch industry.

Just the simple expedient of obtaining supplies from one supplier to eliminate the risk of variation made a tremendous difference in the auto industry. Steel sheeting used in manufacturing car bodies was found to vary, albeit slightly, in thickness, from different suppliers. By concentrating

---

3   The pareto diagram became quite common at the height of the quality movement and demonstrated that 20% of errors cause 80% of problems. This resulted in the Japanese locating, by means of statistical control, the 20% of causes rather than having a shot gun approach at the elimination of error.

on one supplier and constantly keeping the measurements under statistical control, one substantial source of poor quality was eliminated.

Unfortunately, America never really embraced the work of Deming and I suspect that it was because they never understood that underlying his statistical approach was a deep seated philosophy of respect for the human person. It is all very well to have statistical control but another to have people in place who are trusted to measure variation and use their own initiative to prevent unacceptable variation occurring in production.

Statistical control was one thing, but Deming understood the human side of enterprise and his human philosophy was fundamental to the success of his statistical approach.

We have already had an insight into the Deming philosophy[4] but his contribution has been so great that to write a book about the enduring concepts of management without devoting a segment to this amazing person would be negligent.

We come across those books that promote the six easy ways or the ten sure things etc as though management can be reduced to a "tick a box" process[5]. Deming on the other hand came up with fourteen points. He didn't say that these were the only points relevant to successful management, nor did he amplify them, although they are readily understood as a result of his writings[6]. He didn't say that these

---

4   See p. 226.

5   Which is what the Quality Assurance ISO9000 people tried to do with little success.

6   I undertook a course in elementary statistics in order to better understand the works of Deming and my efforts were amply rewarded.

were fourteen points for success or sure fire initiatives that would make you money. No, he simply set out fourteen points for those interested and these underlie his statistical rigour. Without understanding this basic philosophy, statistical control simply becomes another quality assurance programme without a context.

Before moving to these fourteen points it is perhaps worthwhile looking at some examples of their application in the context of statistical control.

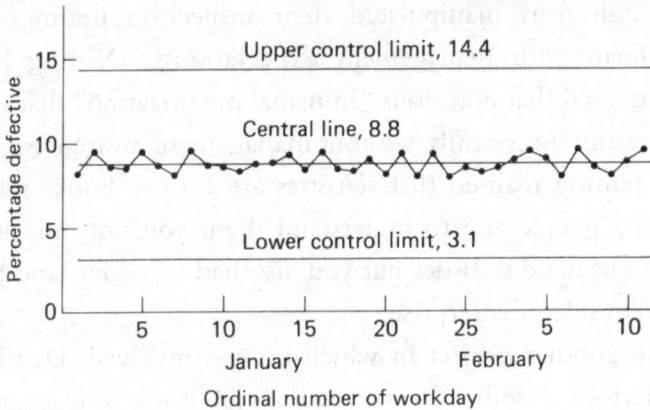

This is a graph[7] prepared by Deming and an associate when called in to examine the proportion of defects found in a final audit prior to shipment of the product. The graph is a record over two months of the percentage of faults per quantity of finished products discovered in the final inspection audit. It will be seen that there is an incredible consistency with little variation. Knowing people and

---

7   W Edwards Deming, *Out of the Crisis,* 18th edn, CUP, 1992, p.265

Graphs on pp. 239 and 240 are used with permission from the publisher, MIT Center for Advanced Engineering Study, Cambridge, MA 02139.

systems as Deming did, he found this persistent statistic over a period of two months to be surprising. In human activities, one expects variation. Normally, Deming would have expected the defects to vary with greater amplitude. So, he said "there is something fishy here!" What he learnt was that senior management had threatened to close the factory if detected defects exceeded ten per cent of product. People doing the inspection and their immediate manager were frightened that many people might lose their jobs if they discovered defects exceeding 10%, and accordingly, through fear, manipulated their inspection findings to conform with management expectations[8]. Deming had discovered that notorious "informal organization" that was operating successfully without management awareness.

Deming realised that statistics are history books written by people and to understand them you not only had to understand statistics but you also had to understand the human side of enterprise.

In another project in which he was involved, Deming undertook a study of women whose job it was to place specific pages of a document in specific pigeon holes according

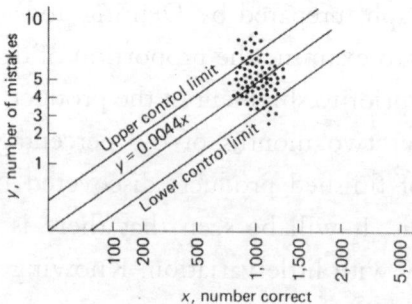

---

8   You might recall the discussion of the Bank Wiring Room experiment in the discussion of the Hawthorne experiments see p. 37 et seq.

to what was printed on the page. There were eighty pigeon holes. Following is the graph[9] Deming constructed:

The graph plots the number of mistakes per worker as against the number of correct placements. You can see that there were a number of workers whose mistakes were beyond what is statistically called "the upper control limit" and a number below the lower control limit, while most were within so called statistical control.

What often happens when someone is not performing as well as someone else is that the poorer performers are considered incompetent and are frequently replaced with other workers. When something goes wrong we are always looking for someone to blame. Deming, before jumping to any conclusions, always undertook a statistical study of the system. There were several reasons for this. One was his belief that everyone going to work is generally trying to do their best, and if they are not successful, it is not for want of endeavour on their part and it is more likely to do with the system in which they are working. Another reason is that there is a statistical tool which tends to compensate for workers who are held up by difficult customers, unusual circumstances or who might be affected by illness or some external and temporary social issue such as a domestic difficulty or the death of a close friend or relative. In such circumstances, people don't work as well as they do in normal circumstances. Rather than marking people according to the average, this statistical tool enables the statistician to see whether a person is within a range that could be expected of them. The tool is called a Standard deviation which provides for upper and lower limits of tolerance. People

9   W Edwards Deming, *Out of the Crisis,* 18th edn, CUP, 1992, p. 259.

working within these upper and lower limits are said to be in statistical control.

You will see in the above graph that there are some women who are above the acceptable statistical limit and some who are below, but the majority are within control. In this case, the immediate response of management was to get rid of the women who were above the upper control limit because they were making more mistakes than was acceptable. Deming said "Hang on a minute; let us look more closely at the problem". He realised that the women who were above the upper control limit were human beings and probably doing their best. He made some inquiries and it turned out that excellent reading skills were necessary in order to identify the different characteristics of the different documents, but that not any of the women had been tested for reading. People with Dyslexia are quite normal people but would be unsuited to this particular type of work. However, they will almost certainly be suitable for other work. He also found that some of the pigeon holes were out of reach of some of the women and they made mistakes reaching for the pigeon holes.

He pointed out that if management altered the system, it would result in the opportunity to improve productivity across the board. Deming kept making the point that if management wanted to improve productivity when the system in operation in the business was in statistical control, the only way to do so would be to alter the system. Exhorting people to do better or sending them on motivational courses or offering them financial incentives would not make any fundamental difference to productivity. According to Deming, the effectiveness of the system in enabling people to do their best is the major determinant of productivity.

Many a person's job would have been retained if management, bent on sacking people for incompetence, had applied some of Deming's philosophy and statistical approach. That is not to mention the enormous improvement in productivity that is possible if, instead of constantly exhorting people to do better and trying to get them to improve productivity by means of financial incentives, management concentrated more on making the system work better for people. You might recall that in the Hawthorne experiments it was discovered that financial incentives had little influence on productivity and not as much as creating the opportunity to achieve worthwhile social benefits[10].

Deming's philosophy embraced the concept that statistically, if something goes wrong, it is more likely to be the failure of the system than the malevolence of the individual. As a product of this philosophy he invented what he called the PDCA circle of constant improvement. PDCA stands for Plan, Do, Check, Act.

Deming used this circle to demonstrate his point. In the first segment of the circle he asks people to plan what they are going to do. Once they have planned it, he wants people to do what they have planned. A lot of people feel diffident when it comes to the doing stage. It is one thing to

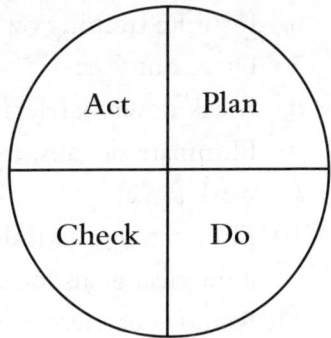

---

10 See Chapter 6. The coincidence of Deming's findings and those of the researchers in the Hawthorne experiments are too compelling to take lightly.

have an idea and another to have the courage to put it into operation. One of Deming's points is to drive out the fear of failure. In order to help people avoid this fear he says that once you have implemented your plan, check to see if it is working. To the extent that it isn't, act on what you have found and once you do that, start the process again so that you are constantly trying to improve the system.

Now, Deming's fourteen points are as follows: (I will provide some explanation of the more important ones).

1. Create constancy of purpose for improvement of product and service;
2. Adopt the new philosophy;
3. Cease dependence on inspection to achieve quality;
4. End the practice of awarding business on the basis of price alone. Instead, minimise total cost by working with a single supplier;
5. Improve constantly and forever every process of planning, production and service;
6. Institute training on the job;
7. Drive out fear;
8. Break down barriers between staff areas;
9. Eliminate slogans, exhortations, and targets for the work force;
10. Eliminate numerical quotas for the work force and numerical goals for management;
11. Remove barriers that rob people of pride in their workmanship. Eliminate the annual rating or merit system;
12. Institute a vigorous programme of education and self-improvement for everyone;

13. Put everybody in the company to work to accomplish the transformation.

You might recall that in Chapter 6[11] I mentioned Drucker's comment that one way of satisfying the innate social conscience of the worker was to create an urgent social purpose for the work such as that which existed in the war. This is exactly what Deming had in mind when he talked about creating a constancy of purpose. Deming believed that this could be achieved by including everyone in the socially beneficial work of constantly improving quality in the USA so that industry in that country could come out of the crisis of lack of competitiveness that beleaguered American industry. If people could see their role as helping America re-emerge as a leading industrial power, it is more likely that they would identify with a constancy of purpose to achieve ever higher levels of quality. Even if people didn't see the wider social benefit for America, but saw in their work that they were constantly attempting to bring to the public better and better products at reduced prices, they would be able to identify with this social benefit. More deeply, Deming realised that competition involved constantly improving the value of the benefits to be conferred on the customer, and that this is central to industrial and financial success.

Ceasing dependence on inspection on the face of it seems to fly in the face of quality assurance. How on earth do you ensure quality if you don't inspect? Deming believed that it was too late to pick up mistakes in the end product, which is generally where inspection identifies them. All the cost has gone by the time the product gets to the inspection stage.

11 See pp. 64–65.

Introducing systemic processes that guaranteed quality and that are designed to eliminate mistakes in production is central to the Deming philosophy. He demonstrated in Japan that this can be done by a combination of his fourteen points, the use of control charts and the education of people at the coal face to identify problems before they find their way into manufacture[12]. That is why for years, people on the floor of the Toyota factory in Nagoya, Japan, have the power to stop production when they identify that something is not quite right. The Nagoya factory is enormous and the production line handles five different model cars at the same time. Can you imagine a worker on the floor pushing a button and stopping production? I have seen it happen and as soon as it does a team descends upon the location of the worker and examines the concerns that gave rise to the stopping of production.

How often do industries trust workers to learn on the job? According to Deming, this is where you have to learn, and while you can learn all sorts of things in a classroom or a training programme, people have to come to understand where the action is. Of course, you don't throw them in at the deep end, but you do give people responsibility to learn on the job and don't blame them for making mistakes when they are learning. In this way, people's natural lack of self-confidence is overcome by supporting them there and then on the job.

---

12 Deming also insisted on spending time in design so as to eliminate mistakes at that stage. There is a rule of thumb in Japanese Quality Control that is summarised in the mathematical statement 1 : 24: 96. Which says that a dollar spent in design will save the expenditure of $24 which it would cost if the mistake was not discovered until the manufacturing stage and $96 if the mistake gets into the market place.

Fear is a devastating condition in any environment and prevents many people achieving their potential. How often has a question been asked and we believe we know the answer but are too frightened to volunteer the answer in public for fear that we might be wrong and make a fool of ourselves? How often in the work place do we think that we have a better idea as to how to do something but keep it to ourselves because we believe that the boss must know what he or she is doing? How often do we think "I should have…" or "I wish I had done or said…"? Fear of making a fool of ourselves, fear of being wrong or simply fear of failure holds so many people back on so many occasions that Deming recognised the condition as endemic in industry and a real constraint on progress and constant improvement. How many suggestion boxes do we see but never put in a suggestion? At the Toyota Factory in Nagoya, approximately 500,000 suggestions are made in a year and many of them are acted upon. Without all the people in an organization embracing the "new philosophy" the ability to constantly improve is constrained and this places organizations at a competitive disadvantage, because without constant improvement, they are at a competitive disadvantage in that they are unable to bring enhanced benefits to their customers at competitive prices.

Just think of the dramatic alteration in the video camera recording industry in the past twenty years. Cam recorders were massive things when they first came on the market and cost a huge amount of money. Today, even the simplest camera has more features than the original cameras and can fit in your pocket and cost pocket money. The industry has driven improvement to the point that there is an abundance of supply chasing an abundant market. Just about anyone can own a camcorder today when once it was the domain of the relatively well-off. This is a result of Deming's philosophy of constant improvement and part of that philosophy is to drive out the fear of failure.

In the hierarchical structures that are central to western organizations, there is a tendency to accept that management tells and staff do. That is a contradiction of Deming's philosophy, which assumes a state where everyone has a part to play in constant improvement and that involves the necessity for management to open up the door to the wealth of experience, knowledge and emotional energy that exists in all of the people in an organization.

Perhaps unwittingly, and from the perspective of a statistician, Deming defined the characteristics of leadership. In this context, it is interesting to examine some of his other points. "Break down barriers between staff areas" is an invitation to open up the workplace so that there are no barriers to communication, whether it be from staff to management or from management to staff. Too often, "communication" consists of edicts issued from above that find their way into the organization by unilateral pronouncements from above, rather than as a result of rich collaboration across the organization. This process often results in the emergence of the "informal organization" as was the case in the example of the consistency of faulty parts inspection mentioned earlier in this chapter.

Deming identified, as did the experimenters at Hawthorne eighty years ago, that informal organizations can be a frightful friction dragging on the performance of an organization and adversely affecting its capacity to constantly enhance the benefits for customers at ever reducing price.

Deming realised that there was a direct correlation between increased quality and reduced cost. He foreshadowed Michael Porter's theory of cost leadership and commenced the process, now gaining momentum, of seeking to get cost and price down to a level that makes it possible to produce goods in abundance and make them available for an abundant audience.

Deming did influence segments of Japanese industry in a profound way and his influence is ongoing. He was not nearly as successful in America, where his book lies on the bookshelves of management schools gathering dust. It is therefore not surprising that in the little town of Williams in Arizona, a high percentage of cars that pass through the intersection by a café are Japanese. Nevertheless, Deming would be pleased that in the April 2010 edition of the Harvard Business Review there are a number of articles in relation to leadership in the medical industry. The articles see the first signs of an awakening in the American medical industry of a need for constant improvement based upon collaboration across the various branches of the industry and a breaking down of the crippling hierarchical culture that has so long dominated the industry. There is even a reference to the use of a Toyota quality system (the modern iteration of Deming's philosophy) in the elimination of infection[13] .

---

13 See article by Professor Richard Bohmer at p. 64 "...some hospitals have applied principles of the Toyota Production System to perfect the technique for placing a central venous line. This has allowed them to reduce the infection rate to zero". I wonder how many lives might have been saved if the medical industry had learnt a bit more about Deming and applied some of his principles?

In another article in the same issue[14], the author bemoans the lethargy of the American medical industry in adopting change and moving to new and innovative collaborative ideas to constantly improve processes that are anchored in the past.

With these signs of an awakening and the return to Deming principles, albeit, without the knowledge or recognition by these avant-garde medical leaders, there is the alarming statistic that while the cost of providing medical services in the USA is the highest in the world and more than twice as high as is the case in Japan, while marginally less high as against the cost in Australia, the fact is that the life expectancy in the USA is lower than in Japan and Australia and lower than all other developed western countries. One ponders the lives that would have been saved, not to mention the cars that would have been sold had the Americans embraced Deming as did the Japanese.

In an unwitting tribute to Deming, another leading medical practitioner in the same issue of the HBR[15] commented:

> *"Think of Sully Sullenberger, the pilot who landed that plane on the Hudson River. The way the public saw him was similar to how it wants to see doctors, and how doctors want to see themselves. The story the public had about him was that he was an unbelievable pilot, and that's what saved the plane. He was the hero.*

---

14 Dr Thomas Lee at pp. 51–58 identifies one medical institution in the USA that sends its prospective leaders to Japan for a two week course in the Toyota Production System.

15 Dr Atul Gawande at p. 61.

*But he kept saying no, it was adherence to
protocol and teamwork that allowed us to safely
land the plane. Heroism in medicine ought to
mean having the humility to recognise that we
are more likely to fail on our own, and embracing
teamwork to help us provide the best care."*

We have a long way to go in the pursuit of customer satisfaction in many areas of activity but Deming provided some critical sign posts that sadly have not been maintained with the result that we have to relearn his message.

While a resident fellow at Thunderbird[16] I presumed to a certain extent on the privilege that the Faculty had extended to me by inviting me there. As my stay on campus was coming to an end, I invited the wonderful Dean of the Faculty to lunch and took with me Deming's book *Out of the Crisis*. I pointed out that the evidence suggested that it has not been utilised in the school and made a plea to the Dean to resurrect Deming as one of the great American management thinkers.

One of the barriers to the adoption of Deming philosophy is that it requires a huge amount of humility. Someone lower down in the order of things might have a better idea and, my goodness, that is a threat to me as a manager as I am supposed to come up with the ideas. Lack of humility creates barriers, which is precisely what Deming wanted to avoid, and barriers create the informal organization which is why Japanese cars are continually driving through a little intersection in Williams AZ and millions of other intersections around the world.

---

16 Thunderbird School of Global Management.

It is my view that no one should aspire to teach any aspect of management to students without deep familiarity with Deming's work. Deming was more than a statistician; he understood the human condition and its potential. Because he had limited literary skills he expressed the beauty of the human condition in statistical format but it is no less potent by reason of that medium. In many countries there are some subjects in school where a seminal book is compulsory reading. I believe that in the United States, *Catcher in the Rye* by JD Salinger is compulsory reading in some English courses and in Italy *The Betrothed*[17] is compulsory reading. *Out of the Crisis* by Deming should be compulsory reading in any business course.

---

17 A Manzoni, *The Betrothed*.

EPILOGUE

It was back in the nineties when I was attending a programme at the University of California (Riverside) that I first came across the dramatic breakthrough in managerial thinking. In one breathtaking stroke of rhetoric, the theory and the purpose of the corporation was reinvented and in terminology that could not be mistaken by CEO's and investors. There, as large as life in the lecture theatre was a lecturer who has become a dear friend, announcing the new paradigm as though its discovery equalled that of Cortez when he discovered the Pacific Ocean. "The purpose of the corporation" my friend proclaimed "is to enhance shareholder value".[1] Besotted by his elegant oratory, I succumbed on the spot only to be troubled a little later when my memory of my legal training, particularly in the area of professional conduct, challenged this concept.

As a young lawyer, I was taught that the principal duty of the lawyer was to act in the best interests of the client. It

---

1   In a lecture to the International Marketing class at the International Extension, UCR by the then Associate Professor in Marketing at the Anderson School of Management, Riverside CA, Professor Sunil Erevelles.

254 • THE 6-HOUR MBA

certainly had nothing to do with improving the bank balance of the owners of the legal practice, although in those days, long since gone and treasured, it was understood rather than expressed that if a lawyer dutifully and ethically acted in the best interest of the client, financial benefits would flow, not, mind you, in the millions now on the table in many legal issues, but sufficient for a more than modest existence.

When challenged with this new and exciting concept that has subsequently wrecked many companies and sent CEO's to prison, I had to deal with what on the surface appeared to be a conflict. As I wrestled with that conflict of shareholder interest versus that of the customer, I gradually had to dissociate myself from the new wisdom and fight a rear guard action in favour of the customer.

This book has attempted to discuss many of the more enduring aspects of management in relation to achieving sustainability in business and I am sure that the reader will have not come across the single-minded pursuit of shareholder value as one of those enduring concepts. The reason that you won't find that pearl of wisdom is that it has absolutely no enduring qualities and its pursuit has caused untold havoc in the commercial world and irremediable damage to ordinary people who have lost their jobs, their homes and often their families in the wake of the blind pursuit of management to enhance shareholder value so that next quarter's stock options will enhance the CEO's personal balance sheet.

I have often asked people why they are in business, and on occasions, the response is "to make money". I can say that almost without fail, those people have not been successful.

If anyone takes anything from this book I would hope that there are at least three concepts that are included in the list.

The first is that the purpose of a business is to bring to the community, benefits that confer value on the purchaser equal to or greater than the value of the money that is paid for those benefits.

The second is that people in the work place are no different to people in the wider community and they yearn for recognition and to achieve self-respect. They ache to contribute in the fullest possible way, their knowledge, experience and emotions to the purpose of the enterprise, and are diminished to the extent that they are ignored or demeaned. Work can be a noble undertaking and occupies the major part of the waking day of individuals. One function of management is to ensure, to the greatest possible extent, that employees have the opportunity to achieve nobility.

The third is that cash is not something to be taken for granted or played with as we would in the game of monopoly. Honestly generated cash should be treated with enormous respect because without it, corporations and their employees cannot survive. Creating surplus cash by single-mindedly pursuing the interest of the customer and responding to the emotional needs of employees is the principle purpose of the corporation. If it is done honestly, ethically and with the best interest of the customers and employees as the primary responsibility of the corporation, then it is as inevitable as the sun rising in the morning that patient shareholders will be rewarded.

Louis A Coutts

INDEX

abundance and scarcity, 128
abundance chasing abundance, 131
accrual accounting, 40, 41, 42
activity cost driver, 147, 148
Adam Smith, 5, 24, 113, 119, 132
Airbus, 79, 83, 85, 86, 87, 88, 89, 90, 91, 92, 93, 154
Argyris, 175, 183
Aristarchus, 1
balance sheet, 42, 43, 44, 46, 47, 49, 50, 51, 53, 201, 207, 208, 211, 212, 213, 214, 215, 216, 220, 257
Balance Sheet, 47, 220
bank wiring room, 57, 61, 68, 224
Barnard, 67, 68, 69, 70, 77, 79, 175, 223
benefits, 12, 19, 22, 23, 24, 25, 27, 28, 30, 31, 33, 35, 36, 73, 96, 112, 116, 118, 119, 121, 122, 125, 126, 132, 134, 141, 142, 143, 145, 149, 169, 173, 188, 203, 204, 210, 215, 233, 245, 248, 250, 251, 256, 257
Bermuda Triangle, 136, 138, 156
Bernabe, 185, 186
billable hours, 169
Boeing, 79, 81, 82, 83, 84, 85, 86, 87, 88, 89, 90, 91, 92, 93, 94, 154, 158, 183, 187, 194
borrowing, 13, 15, 43, 47, 200, 201, 202, 203, 207, 208, 209, 214
borrowings, 7, 13, 14, 47, 202, 204, 208, 209, 210
budgeting, 162, 163, 167, 169
capital, 29, 47, 150, 206, 207, 208, 209
Carlzon, 99, 122, 123, 124
cash, 11, 12, 13, 14, 18, 20, 22, 28, 40, 41, 42, 43, 46, 47, 49, 51, 52, 53, 115, 116, 180, 190, 201, 202, 203, 205, 206, 208, 209, 211, 212, 213, 215, 217, 219, 220, 221, 222, 258
Cash, 11, 12, 49, 53
cash business cycle, 12, 13, 14, 49, 115
cash flow problem, 12, 46, 47, 201
Change, 223
Churchill, 184
Clarence Saunders, 17, 31, 124
competitive advantage, 24, 146, 148, 149, 220, 222
Concorde,, 81
Conferred authority, 173

Cook, 115, 116, 117, 120, 121
Copernicus, 2
Cost leadership, 111, 146
credit, 17, 40, 52, 53, 180, 183, 200, 203, 211, 215, 225, 226
customers, 4, 12, 14, 18, 19, 22, 25, 27, 40, 47, 50, 51, 79, 92, 93, 96, 97, 98, 103, 106, 110, 121, 122, 123, 125, 127, 130, 136, 137, 138, 139, 141, 149, 154, 155, 156, 157, 158, 166, 167, 173, 176, 203, 206, 210, 212, 213, 215, 231, 244, 250, 251, 258
De Havilland, 81
debtors, 44, 51, 52, 211, 212, 213, 214, 215, 216
Debtors, 43, 47, 53, 211
Deming, 23, 105, 230, 231, 237, 238, 239, 240, 241, 242, 243, 244, 245, 246, 247, 248, 249, 250, 251, 252, 253, 254
depreciation, 201, 217, 218, 219, 220, 222
Differentiation, 111, 112, 146
Drucker, 56, 63, 64, 65, 70, 77, 79, 102, 122, 175, 183, 184, 224, 238, 247
Duplesses, 110
Earned authority, 173, 189
Elton Mayo, 55, 59
employees, 3, 14, 27, 73, 79, 84, 85, 86, 87, 91, 92, 93, 124, 141, 151, 152, 153, 155, 166, 173, 175, 176, 177, 182, 183, 188, 189, 190, 195, 226, 232, 233, 258
ENI, 185
Enron, 40, 45, 46, 49, 119, 223, 228
exchange, 17, 19, 22, 23, 24, 25, 27, 28, 30, 31, 33, 36, 38, 77, 96, 97, 113, 115, 116, 129, 208, 214

feedback, 101, 153, 166, 181, 193
Fixed costs, 150
fourteen points, 241, 246, 248
Frederick Winslow Taylor, 3, 56, 102, 172
friction, 76, 77, 141, 194, 251
Friction, 76, 77
Fritz Jules Roethlisberger, 55
frustration, 6, 48, 78, 178, 194, 195, 197, 224
frustrations, 48, 78, 79, 194, 226
Galileo, 2
General Motors, 28, 56, 63, 184, 238
goodwill, 36, 37, 38, 103, 174
Google, 7, 117, 118, 120, 130, 135, 139
Greyhound, 125, 204
Gutenberg, 20, 21
Harvard School of Industrial Psychology, 55, 57
Hawthorne experiments, 8, 57, 68, 102, 223, 224, 232, 242, 245
Human Resources, 3
Human side of enterprise, 56, 59, 175
informal organization, 58, 68, 73, 103, 187, 189, 190, 202, 224, 233, 242, 251, 254
Internal Revenue Authority, 40
Iridium, 99, 107, 108
J C Penney's, 37
Kottler, 23
law of supply and demand, 5, 7, 128, 130, 131, 135, 139
layoffs, 4, 89, 92, 194
leadership, 103, 112, 146, 153, 171, 172, 173, 175, 176, 178, 180, 183, 186, 187, 188, 189, 191, 250, 251, 252
Lester Thurow, 84

loan, 45, 116, 200, 203, 205, 206, 207
Lockheed, 82
Madhoff, 119
marginal cost, 151, 152, 153, 158
marginal costs, 154, 156, 158, 162, 166
Market research, 108
marketing, 22, 23, 34, 95, 96, 98, 99, 100, 102, 103, 105, 110, 111, 113, 114, 115, 116, 117, 118, 119, 120, 122, 124, 125, 126, 128, 129, 132, 135, 145, 233
Maslow, 65, 66, 70, 73, 74, 77, 120, 175, 194, 197, 227
McDonald Douglas, 82
McGregor, 56, 70, 71, 72, 77, 79, 175, 189, 195, 196, 198, 224
Merrill Lynch, 18, 28
Microsoft, 118
Mixed costs, 150
Moments of Truth, 99, 123
Motivation and Personality, 65, 175, 194, 197
Motorola, 99, 106, 107, 108
Mulally, 187
needs, 7, 33, 48, 59, 65, 66, 70, 72, 73, 77, 80, 103, 106, 110, 114, 116, 120, 121, 122, 126, 133, 152, 156, 173, 174, 175, 176, 190, 195, 196, 197, 227, 258
negative cash flow, 13
Newhouse, 86, 88, 89, 90, 92
News Corporation, 200
Niche markets, 111, 146
non-value adding activity, 143
organizational effectiveness, 99, 101, 103, 112, 134, 135
Panama Canal, 110
Pareto, 239
PDCA circle, 246

physics, 75, 76
Piggly Wiggly stores, 19
positive cash flow, 14, 49, 53, 206, 219
potential energy, 75, 76, 77
price, 5, 18, 20, 22, 24, 29, 30, 34, 35, 36, 37, 38, 40, 45, 89, 91, 112, 114, 115, 116, 117, 118, 120, 121, 122, 127, 129, 130, 131, 134, 135, 136, 138, 139, 141, 143, 144, 147, 148, 149, 173, 177, 179, 190, 202, 204, 210, 220, 246, 251
price elasticity, 5, 135, 136, 137, 139
Principles of Scientific Management, 56, 102, 172
productivity, 3, 8, 56, 57, 58, 60, 61, 64, 72, 74, 79, 101, 102, 122, 137, 145, 153, 180, 194, 245
profit, 12, 28, 29, 33, 35, 41, 42, 43, 44, 45, 46, 49, 50, 51, 52, 80, 92, 93, 96, 115, 121, 122, 130, 131, 135, 137, 139, 143, 144, 147, 149, 155, 156, 178, 179, 202, 210, 212, 217, 218, 224
profit and loss account, 41, 43, 44, 49, 50, 52, 149, 217, 218
Profit and Loss account, 41, 43, 44, 46
Ptolemy, 1, 2, 8
quality, 5, 7, 8, 24, 35, 47, 98, 99, 100, 103, 110, 128, 132, 138, 140, 147, 174, 178, 215, 230, 239, 240, 241, 246, 247, 248, 251, 252
Range costs, 151
range of activity, 152, 153, 162, 168, 169
Resources graph, 156
ROI, 29
SAS, 122, 123, 124
self-esteem, 67, 73, 101, 195, 198

self-service grocery, 17
service, 7, 12, 17, 24, 71, 82, 114, 123, 124, 135, 145, 148, 151, 156, 157, 185, 201, 202, 203, 204, 205, 206, 209, 210, 230, 246
shareholder interest, 29, 256
shareholder value, 4, 5, 7, 27, 28, 80, 209, 210, 256, 257
shareholders, 84, 93, 207, 208, 258
Shewart, 239
South West airlines, 79
South West Airlines, 92, 127
staff, 48, 54, 79, 80, 87, 89, 90, 91, 124, 155, 156, 167, 176, 178, 180, 181, 182, 189, 190, 191, 193, 194, 195, 220, 226, 228, 247, 250
step-up syndrome, 158
Steve Jobs, 181, 189
stock, 17, 18, 19, 22, 33, 36, 50, 52, 53, 92, 129, 208, 215, 257
supermarket, 20, 30, 31, 100, 105, 124
suppliers, 14, 25, 27, 88, 94, 134, 147, 171, 176, 214, 240
sustainable business, 22, 23, 36, 134
Swiss watch industry, 146
tax department, 41
Taylorism, 3, 56, 102
Telecom Italia, 186
The functions of the Executive, 67
The Hawthorne Experiments, 55
the relay assembly room, 60, 61, 62
Theory X, 71, 72, 196, 198
Theory Y, 71, 196
Thomas Cook, 115, 116, 118, 120
Total Quality Control, 225
Total Quality Management, 109, 225, 226

value adding activity, 143
value chain, 124
Variable costs, 149
Vickers Corporation, 81
Victoria Market, 30
Western Electric, 55, 57, 59
William J Dixon, 55
World War II, 63

ABOUT THE AUTHOR

Louis A Coutts was a litigation lawyer and is now a management consultant. He studied management at various American Universities including Stanford, Colombia, Kellogg and the University of California. He has consulted for many companies and has acted in the capacity of CEO in turnaround situations.

He has become intimately acquainted with issues in the work place that prevent people and organizations (including not for profit) achieving their potential. Through these findings he has written widely on management issues with columns featured in *Management Today*, *BRW*, smartcompany.com.au.

His earlier works on "Computers and the law" achieved international recognition and he has presented to international conferences including the International Law Association and the Australasian Society of Radiology.

He has been a visiting lecturer at the University of California and the University of the Pacific in California as well as a visiting Fellow at Thunderbird Global School of Management and has been invited this year as a Fellow at the Weatherhead School of Management at Case Western Reserve in Cleveland Ohio. Both of these institutions are in the top one hundred business schools in the world. For some years he was a member of the online Council of the Harvard Business Review.

Louis founded the Hawthorne Academy which provides practical courses in different aspects of business, concentrating on the potential of individuals. He is a member of the International Commission of Jurists and as such has published technical material in relation to the constraints on the power of legislators such as the Federal Government.

		QTY
The 6-hour MBA	$26.99	....

Postage within Australia (1 book) $5.00   ....
Postage within Australia (2 or more books) $9.00   ....

TOTAL* $_____

* All prices include GST

Name: ....

Address: ....

Phone: ....

Email Address: ....

Payment:
❑ Money Order ❑ Cheque ❑ Amex ❑ MasterCard ❑ Visa

Cardholder's Name:..

Credit Card Number: ....

Signature:...

Expiry Date: ....

Allow 21 days for delivery.

Payment to: Better Bookshop (ABN 14 067 257 390)
PO Box 12544
A'Beckett Street, Melbourne, 8006
Victoria, Australia
Fax: +61 3 9671 4730
betterbookshop@brolgapublishing.com.au

BE PUBLISHED

Publishing through a successful Australian publisher. Brolga provides:
- Editorial appraisal
- Cover design
- Typesetting
- Printing
- Author promotion
- National book trade distribution, including sales, marketing and distribution through Macmillan Australia.

For details and inquiries, contact:
Brolga Publishing Pty Ltd
PO Box 12544
A'Beckett St VIC 8006

Phone: 03 9600 4982
bepublished@brolgapublishing.com.au
markzocchi@brolgapublishing.com.au
ABN: 46 063 962 443